What to Eat When You're Broke

What to Eat When You're Broke

A Frugal Food Philosophy for Eating WELL on a Tiny Budget

Daisy Luther

Banned Books Publishing

Cheyenne, Wyoming

Contents

Everyone is trying to save money right now. For some, it's optional, and for others, it's the only way to survive. One place where nearly everybody can slash costs is in the kitchen. You don't have to be a gourmet chef to do this in a tasty way that everyone in your household will enjoy. In fact, you can be lazy as heck and still save money.

If you are a reader of my website, The Frugalite, you know that our motto over there is "live large on a tiny budget." We like to have fun experiences, decorate beautiful homes, spend time with our loved ones, and have nice things. We just don't want to go broke doing it, and we prioritize our spending. We choose where to make cuts so we can also choose where to spend a bit more.

The motto of this book, in true Frugalite spirit, could be "eat well on an itty-bitty grocery bill." I'd say "eat large" but eating large sounds like we're auditioning for one of those reality shows with a person who weighs a thousand pounds, and that, my friends, could not possibly be frugal.

Anywhooo.

Whether you're dumpster-diving-for-food poor, have an incredibly limited grocery budget, or a garden variety thrifty grocery budget, you'll find some ideas that work for you. Most of the suggestions also consider that someone with a tight budget probably spends a lot of time working and can't always deliver every single bite from lengthy scratch-cooking processes.

This can't really be called a cookbook as much as it is a "hodgepodge of thrifty ideas about food." I don't have measurements for most of them because I'm a "fling things together" cook. You can substitute ingredients in just about every so-called recipe based on what you have on hand. The flexibility is what helps to make it so frugal. These foods are truly YOUR meals, based on what you have, what you'll eat, and what you can afford.

The meals can be as healthy or unhealthy as the ingredients you choose. If you have a pristine kitchen into which a non-organic food or canned good has never once crossed the organic-vinegar-mopped threshold, you can still make many of these dishes, but they won't be thrifty.

The same thing goes for those of you who cook purely from scratch. There are a lot of shortcuts here because time is money too. If your choice is between taking 3 hours to make a scratch meal or ordering pizza, I vote that you use the shortcuts and take your kid to basketball practice, for crying out loud. So, you'll find that some meals could have been thriftier, but I went for time-saving choices too.

All that being said, let's get started.

Bon Appe-Cheap!

Frugalicious Philosophies

One of the easiest places to cut spending is with food, even in these days of high inflation and concerning economic issues. But a lot of folks approach things all wrong. They look strictly for cheap recipes and don't pay enough attention to the philosophies of eating when you're broke.

But eating well (or at least decently) when you're short on cash is about mindset in so many ways. It's not just about saving money on one meal. It's about saving across the board and changing your habits to ones that fit your new budget.

Disclaimer: Let me be absolutely clear that if you have a serious health problem such as celiac disease, diabetes, or Crohn's, just to name a few, do not go and willy-nilly add things that make you sick into your diet, even to save money. If you have a health concern that means you need a special diet, do your best to adapt the strategies in this book to work with your plan. You cannot adapt your body to work with the book as it's written. And always contact your doctor before making major dietary changes.

I think it can all boil down to ten concepts. Ten commandments, if you will, to borrow a phrase from that super-famous book. If you master these philosophies, you will automatically make the best choices possible.

When I took these things to heart, everything changed for me. Not only did we have nice, balanced meals regardless of what was going on, but I got better at planning ahead. And I'm not just talking about planning ahead as in what's for dinner, but for the entire week, month, or even further in advance. And you know what? I actually *enjoyed* it. I loved what I was doing and I felt good about it.

Here are my own rules of what to eat when you're broke.

Verily I say unto you, thou shalt learn to freaking cook.

Okay, I'm not telling you that you have to go out there and hit up your nearest Le Cordon Bleu Academy. There are simply some very basic, very easy things that you need to master if you want to eat decently without spending a fortune. To name a few things:

Measure

If you are following a specific recipe or baking, you need to know how to measure. You can easily acquire measuring cups and measuring spoons to help you with this. Pretty soon, for regular cooking, you'll be able to eyeball most things.

Brown/Saute

This refers to heating up a fat (oil or shortening or butter) on a skillet and dropping in some diced-up veggies or meat in the pan to lightly cook it and make it a golden color.

Bake

Literally, turn on your oven to the appropriate temperature, preheat it until it reaches that temperature, put in what you're cooking, and take out the food at the prescribed time. That leads us to...

Use a timer

Trust me on this one – your life will be much easier and more oops-free if you make a habit of setting a timer before you walk away from food that is cooking or baking. I set them to remind me to stir and to remind me to take them off the burner.

Read

I'm not being snarky here. (Okay, I'm always snarky, but not in a mean way.) If you can follow the steps above and read the instructions, you *can* cook.

Use a crock pot

If you don't have a crock pot, stop what you're doing and get one *right-freaking-now*. I'll wait here while you order it. There is literally no easier way to make a hearty homemade meal with minimal effort. I know everyone has instant pots now, but I still love my crock pot.

Look, you're going to make some mistakes at first, and that's all part of the process. Every time you do, you've learned what does not work, and you won't do it again. You *can* do this. I promise. You. Can. Do. This.

Thou shalt select carefully the fish, fowl, beast, and product of the fields upon which thou spendeth thy money.

When money is tight, you can't just hie yourself off to the most expensive, luxurious grocery store in town. You need to consider which stores have the most things at the lowest price. One way to comparison-shop is to use an app like Instacart. No, you're not going to spend the $10-20 premium to have things delivered. You're going to build identical carts at multiple nearby stores and see where you can accomplish your shopping the least expensively.

For me, that's nearly always Aldi, Food Lion, or Walmart. This is very regional, so you'll have to figure out your local "cheap" store.

As well, understand that your diet may look a little different than it normally does. Remember, your goal is to get through the week or month without going hungry, not to go organic-gluten-free-paleo-keto-vegan.

Look at lower priced options such as conventional over organic, ingredients instead of ready-meals, and canned or frozen instead of fresh.

Thou shalt not wasteth the food that remaineth after thou dine.

For the love of all things cute and fluffy, stop wasting food.

That means you need to eat leftovers. You need to dish out smaller servings and let people get seconds instead of scraping waste into the trash. You need to put food away in a way that it won't spoil before you can eat it. You need to store groceries in a manner to prevent them from becoming stale or rotting. Don't forget to eat things before they spoil or expire.

We've got LOADS of ideas coming up for ways to stop food waste!

Thou shalt buildeth a larder from which thou shalt dine during difficult times.

You can build your own food bank right there in your house if you shop wisely. If you see non-perishable goods on sale, grab those suckers and put them back. I'm talking about canned goods, larger bags of flour and rice, and dried items like pasta and crackers.

Fill your pantry and cupboards with food that will see you through the long run. You can always supplement your current diet with them, and there's always going to be a time at which you're so so glad you have this food. Another bonus to building a good pantry is that if you have a friend or loved one going through a hard time, you can help.

Buy these things at the lowest possible prices and watch your "best by" dates carefully. Rotate the older items to the front of your cupboard so you don't miss out on eating something by its date.

Thou must plan ahead, so thou dost not goeth through the drive-through, ordereth Door Dash, or taketh thine family to a restaurant or other palace of

expensive food.

One of the biggest reasons I blew my frugal food plan in the past was that I didn't plan ahead. I didn't have something in the crockpot or a prepped food item waiting for my hungry kids to eat after a long day at work, school, and daycare. Or I worked late and couldn't face an hour in the kitchen when McDonald's drive-through was on the way home and would only take five minutes.

Nearly all of those impromptu splurges can be eliminated with good planning and prep.

Let me be clear – I'm not saying you can never ever eat out again. I'm just suggesting you plan it and work it into your budget.

Thy time is as important as thy money.

Sometimes all of the things above can be incredibly time-consuming, and time is just as important as money, especially for those with very busy schedules. Have some speedy go-to meals that can be ready in a flash for those days when there's more stuff to do than time in which to do it.

Shortcuts are often a bit more expensive, but they're rarely going to cost more than going out to dinner.

Thou shalt not be a picky eater, nor shalt thou tolerate pickiness.

If there's one thing a family with a tight food budget can't afford, it's a picky eater.

One place where I always held a hard disciplinary line was the dinner table. Our budget was so incredibly tight at times that the very idea of one of my kids refusing to eat whatever I managed to serve was unthinkable. (Sure, I did my best to accommodate favorites and make food they'd enjoy, but as any parent knows, there are hits and misses.)

This is a very personal decision and I'm not going to tell you how you "should" handle it. I'm going to give you the two options of which I'm aware for sticking to your budget with picky eaters in the house and share what I did. How you choose to handle it in your household is totally up to you. Some people will think I'm the world's meanest mom, and others will probably say, "Heck, yeah." You have to decide how to handle this in your family.

And also, keep in mind, your picky person might not be a child. If there's an adult at your table who refuses to eat what is served, you can't exactly order them to eat it and like it. Some of these tips may still be helpful even if it's a grown-up gagging at the idea of eating home-cooked oatmeal.

There are a few reasons that folks who refuse to eat what is served to them can cause issues with your grocery budget:

1. **It's expensive.** There's nothing more distressing to a flat-broke mama than seeing a meal she prepared sit there on the table uneaten while her children rebel against the very idea of it. Not only is it kind of hurtful, but if the meal can't be salvaged and reserved as something more palatable, it's like throwing dollar bills down the garbage disposal.
2. **It makes it harder to experiment**. If you're looking for ways to use your leftovers, like in soups or casseroles, it can be tough to get creative when your efforts are likely to be met with stony refusal.
3. **It's harder to shop the sales**. If your family members will only eat specific brand names, certain cuts of meat, or one type of bread, it's a whole lot harder to go stock up on whatever happens to be discounted during your shopping trip.
4. **It makes it harder for the picky person.** One day, the only things available or affordable could be something far from desirable. it could be a lot more difficult to make the adjustment then than in the

safe, secure surroundings of today. As well it makes it more difficult for them to go out to eat or have dinner at a friend's house.

Picky eating is no picnic for anyone at the table – the chef, the other family members who witness the drama, or the person who doesn't want to eat what's served.

The way I see it, there are only two options: plan your meals around the picky eater or don't allow picky eating. What you choose really depends on who the finicky person is, why they're so particular, and your own level of stubborn determination.

Planning meals around picky eaters

One option to prevent food waste is to plan your meals around the picky eaters in your household. In my opinion, this is the less ideal choice because it means that you can't stock up on and base meals around whatever happens to be on sale. But if you don't think you can convince them to eat the food, or if you aren't willing to do so, then at least this way, everyone gets fed, and groceries don't get wasted.

If you intend to plan your meals around their preferences, make yourself a list of all the things these family members will eat. Create a revolving member consisting of these foods and keep a grocery list of the necessary ingredients in your wallet. Every time you shop look for these itmes on sale and stock up as much as you can on them.

- **Experiment *slightly*.** You can potentially expand their palates a little bit by adding different versions of the same thing. If they prefer one particular kind of chicken nugget, you might be able to make a scratch version that gets close that they'll also consume.
- **Make only meals they like.** You can limit the entire family to the meals that the picky folks eat. If this is the majority of your family, then this could be the easiest solution rather than trying to convert everyone at once.
- **Save the package.** If you have a kiddo who will only use one brand of ketchup (and of course, it's the expensive one) you might try stealthily refilling the empty brand-name bottle with bargain-priced generic ketchup. It's possible they'll never notice.
- **Make them separate meals**. Some families make separate meals for finicky folks. My mother used to make two versions of salad, for example, because my dad would only eat lettuce, onion, croutons, and French dressing in his. Meanwhile, we had a salad with a different dressing and a whole host of vegetables. If everyone else will cooperate with an inexpensive meal, have some low-effort, low-priced

alternatives such as PB&J, grilled cheese, or hot dogs.

These strategies will vary with the families and the reasons.

Or you might choose not to allow picky eating.

As I mentioned above, I was determined that my children not be picky. So I simply didn't allow it.

That may seem overly simplistic if your child has already developed his or her own strongly held preferences. It worked for me because I started it as soon as they could eat food. And I was a big old meanie.

My babies were exposed to a wide range of foods. Once we got past the single ingredient stage, they ate whatever my husband and I were eating in a suitable consistency for their age. So, if I made a lentil and rice casserole, I squished it with a fork, gave them their little spoon, and that was their dinner too. The only things my children didn't like were foods that were "too spicy" so I just used cayenne pepper as a table seasoning like salt and black pepper for the adults. Because they grew up from the time they could chew eating everything, there was never an issue with expanding their palates.

This is not to say there were never any stand-offs at the dinner table. Like anyone, they had preferences. I had a few rules to handle mealtimes.

1. **You have to try one bite.** When something is served, you must try one bite. Just because you didn't like artichoke hearts last year doesn't mean you won't like artichoke hearts this year. (Not that artichoke hearts are overly thrifty – it's just the example that popped into my head.) Just because you don't like mushrooms in spaghetti sauce doesn't mean you won't like them in gravy.

2. **You have to be polite**. If there's something on your plate you don't care for, after trying one bite, you can quietly push it to the side. If you make a scene and yell "ewww" or "this is gross" then you're getting a double serving of it and you're not leaving the dinner table until it's gone. If you still don't eat it, you will have it for breakfast. (This only happened once or twice for each of my girls. When they learn you absolutely mean business, they no longer challenge you on stuff like this. They'll eat their bite, then be happy they were allowed to quietly push it to the side.)

3. **What's for dinner is what's for dinner.** I never made a different meal for my kids. If they didn't care for what was served, they'd nibble at it and follow the rules above. There were no snacks after dinner

except the small one right before bed. (Usually a graham cracker and a small glass of milk) If you didn't like dinner, well, nobody ever died from missing one meal. Generally, they used the "suck it up, buttercup" philosophy because whatever they didn't eat was bound to show up as a leftover at some point in the future, so they might as well get it over with and just eat it the first time.

4. **I made stuff they liked, too.** One night a week, each of my kids got to pick what was going to be for dinner. To keep it budget-friendly, I'd offer them two choices from their favorites, for example, "Do you want vegetable soup and bread, or bean burritos?" Doing this kept them from revolting over the occasional unpopular meal.

5. **We played Crapper or Keeper.** I tried tons of new recipes and experiments over the years, even before I began writing cookbooks and blogging. We played a silly game I called Crapper or Keeper, where we'd vote at the end of the meal whether or not that particular combination should ever be served again. It was a fun way for them to share their likes and dislikes, and have some say in the menu.

You may come to a point at which you have to outlast your child. There are very few kids on the planet who will willingly starve to death to get a chicken nugget instead of chicken soup. They might hang in there for a day or so, but you need to remember, you're the adult and you set the rules. I know it's stressful – one of my stubborn daughters went until dinner the following night refusing to eat a food that she later (in a totally different meal) really enjoyed.

Disallowing picky behavior has benefits that go further than frugality. When my girls were invited to dinner at a friend's house, they politely ate everything they were offered and complimented their host. I nearly always got a comment from the other children's parents about how polite my kids were at the dinner table and how they wished their own would eat as cooperatively. As adults, both of my daughters are excellent, creative cooks and both will eat just about anything – which really helps when they're on tight budgets.

Thou shalt honor thy body by bearing food to thine table which is as delicious and healthy as thou canst make it.

While you may have to tone down the level of quality in the food that you eat during difficult times, that doesn't mean you should resort to nothing but generic Cheetos and ramen packets. You still need to provide as much nutrition and balance as possible in order to stay healthy.

Because let's face it, being sick isn't exactly a thrifty way to spend your time either.

Secondly, it should taste decent. We're not talking about The Russian Tea Room or Tavern on the Green level, but put enough effort into it that your meal is both filling to the stomach and satisfying to the taste buds. You feel so much less deprived eating inexpensively when you produce healthy, hearty, and flavorful fare out of thrifty ingredients.

Thou shalt bringeth thine own food and drink to work and school, so thou dost not falleth into desperation and hunger.

Brown bag lunches aren't just for kids! You can save a fortune each month by bagging up a lunch for the grownups in the family, too. And it isn't only about lunch, either. After-school snacks and meals on-the-go for busy days are a must to stay well-fed without spending unnecessary money.

Years ago, when packing two lunches for the girls each morning, I also packed lunch for myself. I was in a workplace where lunch was a social event for many of my co-workers. Each day, they'd have a long discussion about where to go out to lunch. I went with them a few times but soon saw at least $50 per week drifting away with those fattening, unhealthy meals. That, of course, is $200 a month or $2400 per year – a lot of money for a less-than-stellar meal.

The same goes for school lunches for the kids. A school lunch averages $2.60 across the United States. This works out to $13 per week, $52 per month, and $468 over a school year. PER CHILD. If you have more kids, you'll need to multiply that number again.

So, a quick calculation.

In a family with two adults working outside the home and two children in school, if all of those meals are purchased, you could be looking at a whopping $5,736 per year JUST FOR LUNCHES. Think about what you could do with that extra money each year if you worked lunches into the weekly grocery budget. It could be a vacation, a massive chunk of money paid off of your car loan or mortgage, or a nice cushion in your emergency fund.

Some people say that they don't have the time to pack a brown bag lunch, so here are some tips to make it easier.

Make lunches when you are cleaning up the kitchen after dinner.

Add leftovers to containers you can heat at the office. Put aside a serving to heat in the morning and add to a thermos for the kiddos. Put sliced fruit and veggies into zip-lock bags for snacks. My kids always preferred to assemble their sandwiches at school, so for them, I'd place leftover meat in a zip-lock bag and a bun in another bag.

Prep some of your lunches during your weekly meal prep extravaganza.

Later on in the book, we'll talk about frugal meal prepping. You can portion out treats like cookies, sliced veggies, dip, and salads to grab when you're in a rush. Grabbing lunches will be a snap.

Teach the kids to make their own lunches.

I saw a cute system on Pinterest that brought back memories. You can grab some inexpensive plastic tubs to set up in the fridge with numbers on them. The numbers represent how many items in that tub your child can take in their lunch box. So, for example, 1 protein, 2 veggies, 1 fruit, and 1 treat. If you stock this on Sunday night, the kids will be all set to grab lunches each morning before school quickly.

And don't forget to BYOBeverages

Of course, don't forget how much money you can save by bringing your own beverages, too. Every bottle of <u>water</u> you purchase will run you at least a dollar (or $2). Each drive-thru coffee you grab is going to be anywhere from $2-6, depending on how fancy you get. Even if you end up bringing a can of soda pop with you, it's going to be a fraction of the price if you bring it from home.

Here are a couple of ideas:

- **Reusable water bottles:** get a dishwasher-safe bottle and run it each night with the dinner dishes. Refill it with filtered water from home and store it in the fridge until time to go.
- **Thermoses:** I used to take a big thermos full of coffee, doctored up exactly how I liked it. Then I could indulge all day long at work.
- **Pre-packaged drinks:** Soda pops, juice boxes, bottles of iced tea – they're all cheaper purchased in bulk when you go grocery shopping. And if you

know you're just going to grab it from the vending machine, you might as well bring it from home, right?

If you add the cost of beverages to all of the other "getting food out" expenses, you've easily added another thousand bucks to your budget over the course of the year.

Thou shalt honor the seasons and dineth upon that which is fresh in fields and farms.

Eating in season can do two things for you. It can save you money, and it can make you healthier. If the idea appeals to you, consider starting a small garden this year, even if it's just in some pots on your patio or balcony. This is a great, thrifty source of delicious fresh produce right by your back door. You can also visit your local farmer's market for some great deals. I like to shop near the end of the day and make an offer on all the X they have left. Be polite and don't lowball too much, and you may not just make a great score, you might make a farmer friend too.

If you get your mind right, and your

budget will follow.

Most importantly, you have to get your head right and the steps above can help you. Don't approach this like it's torture. You're not eating prison food. You're just on a budget. Take pride in making delicious meals from thrifty ingredients. Savor your achievements as you learn to make new things and save more money. Make it *fun*, for crying out loud.

This, like everything else, is more about your attitude than anything else.

Flat Broke Grocery Shopping

Have you ever had a time when money is so tight you can't imagine how you're possibly going to feed your family? It's frightening, stressful, and mentally exhausting. Not much is worse, particularly as a parent, as not knowing where your child's next meal is coming from. After all, it's your job as a mom or dad to meet their needs and provide for them.

When your budget is super tight, grocery shopping is going to look a lot different. First of all, you're not going to be able to provide the highest quality ingredients straight from Whole ~~Paycheck~~ – ahem – Whole Foods. Secondly, you might not even be able to buy a lower quality of all the ingredients you want or are used to.

There are a few strategies you can use to shop during times like this.

- Lower your standards.
- Consider different options.
- Create a meal plan and a list (but in pencil, not pen).
- Consider once-a-month shopping.
- Guerilla shopping.

Let's discuss each one.

Lower your standards

Let me reiterate the disclaimer from the last chapter:

If you have a serious health problem such as celiac disease, diabetes, or Crohn's, just to name a few, this advice may not safely apply to you. If you have a health concern that means you need a special diet, do your best to adapt the strategies in this book to work with your plan. You cannot adapt your body to work with the book as it's written. And always contact your doctor before making major dietary changes.

Now, that being said, if you're eating gluten-free because it's trendy or because you kinda sorta might feel better when you don't eat wheat (or pick the food group you avoid and the reason you avoid it), you may need to make changes. Personally, I prefer a moderate carb, organic diet with high protein. I feel my absolute best when I eat that way. But can I do it all the time? Absolutely not. When money is tight, my diet is looser.

So, for example, don't plan on eating low-carb during a rough month. Adding more grains and starches to your diet during a rough spot can really help you through it.

Also, you probably won't be able to eat organic. If you normally eat nothing but fresh, organic goodness, revisit the Dirty Dozen and Clean Sixteen on the EWG website and just try to focus on choices that are drenched in fewer pesticides.

If times are really, really tight, you are going to need to loosen your standards to survive. If you are rock bottom broke, you may have to go even cheaper. So, when I recommend canned fruits and lots of potatoes here in the next section, I don't want to hear, "But that's not heeeeaaaalllthy!" It's also not healthy to eat one really good clean meal every other day because that's all you can afford. In fact, I'd posit that is far less healthy than dropping your standards some.

Just make the best choices you can while still staying fed, okay?

Let's go through our food groups really quickly to give you an idea what you'll be looking for on your shopping trip.

Consider different options to get balance.

None of these lists is comprehensive – you have to go with the things your family will eat and the things you can personally acquire inexpensively. That will be different for everyone.

Protein

When you're broke, protein is going to be the costliest part of your menu.

Meat: When your budget is super tight, don't expect meat to be the main dish. I'm not saying you have to go vegetarian, but calorie for calorie, meat is very expensive. Use less meat than you normally would and make it an ingredient instead of the star of the meal. Go with less expensive cuts and cook them for a long time: stew beef, 70/30 ground beef, chicken quarters, chicken thighs, etc., are much less costly. You can also buy an inexpensive beef roast and an inexpensive whole chicken that will get you through several meals if carefully doled out.

Eggs: Eggs are a less expensive and healthy source of protein. (Even now, as I write this, with skyrocketing egg prices.) Walmart has huge flats with 30 eggs for a very reasonable price. I suggest you grab a few of those and think about breakfast for dinner.

Beans: I absolutely love beans and strongly recommend them. Proper soaking and rinsing can reduce the resulting flatulence that a lot of folks worry about. Go with dried beans instead of canned ones for greater savings. If your family members don't like beans, they might prefer refried beans or bean dip. Worst case scenario, you can puree cooked beans and add them to a soup for a nutrient boost.

Peanut butter: Peanut butter is a tasty protein source, and most kids love it. (Assuming there are no allergies, of course.) Grab a huge jar, and if possible, go for one that is more natural. Skippy and Jif both have a natural peanut butter without a whole lot of additives.

Canned tuna: Beware of eating this stuff non-stop because of high levels of mercury, but some canned tuna will add much-needed protein to your menu.

Lentils and split peas: Both of these are high in protein, dirt cheap, and easy to turn into delicious soups.

Fruits and Vegetables

Produce is a very important part of a healthy diet.

Without it, you're at risk for all sorts of deficiency diseases. When shopping once a month, plan to eat your fresh stuff early in the month and then move on to your frozen or canned goods.

Apples: If the price is reasonable, grab a large bag of apples. This will provide you with some fresh fruit.

Applesauce: This is a great addition for later in the month when the fresh stuff is gone. To save money, look for large jars of applesauce instead of the little individual packets for lunch boxes. Go with unsweetened applesauce.

Canned fruit: Get fruit canned in the lightest syrup possible, or fruit canned in juice. Just because you're broke doesn't mean you need to eat 10 pounds of sugar per day, right? Canned fruit is a nice addition to pancakes, waffles, or oatmeal. Reserve the juice for baking.

Overripe bananas: If your store has a last-day-of-sale bin for produce, you may be able to grab some overripe bananas. Get these and take them home for banana bread.

Carrots: I'm not talking about baby carrots here. I'm talking about those huge bags of grown-up carrots you'll need to peel and slice yourself. Remember that you're either spending time or money. Carrots are a perfect example of that. Peel them, slice them, and keep them in a bowl of water in your fridge for yummy snacking.

Potatoes: A couple of bags of potatoes can get you through a rough time. Potatoes are filling, can be cooked in a lot of different ways, and most folks love them. Leave the peel on for added fiber. Store them in a cool, dark place away from onions for the longest life. Even when they're sprouting eyes, you can eat them, though – just cut out the sprouting parts.

Onions: A big bag of onions will help you flavor up your home cooking this month.

Garlic: Sometimes it's cheaper to buy garlic already chopped up in a jar. Grab enough garlic to spice up your food over the course of the month.

Cabbage: Depending on the time of year, a few heads of cabbage will get you far for very little money. You can use cabbage in coleslaw, salads, soup, or casseroles. You don't need to get fancy – just go with the plain, ordinary green heads of cabbage if they're the cheapest.

Canned tomatoes: My favorite canned good is canned tomatoes. I like to get a variety of crushed and diced ones. These can be used for soups, chili, casseroles, and sauces. Canned tomatoes are a nutritional powerhouse.

Frozen vegetables: At my local grocery store, I can get bags of frozen vegetables for a dollar each, and sometimes less. If you have freezer space, this is the way to go. Our favorites are peas and carrots, green peas, corn, cauliflower, broccoli, chopped spinach, Brussels sprouts, mixed vegetables, and green beans. With an assortment of frozen vegetables, you can make all sorts of great stuff.

Whatever is in season: Every season, there are fruits and veggies that are at their ripest and least expensive. What is in season depends on when your personal financial catastrophe occurs. (More on seasonal eating in the last chapter.)

Dairy

If you consume dairy products on a daily basis, you're going to want to still consume dairy products when times are tough. (Cream for your coffee, milk for cereal, a beverage for the kiddos).

Generic milk by the gallon is your least expensive way to go for this. You can make all sorts of things from your gallons of milk, like homemade yogurt and cottage cheese. I suggest you put aside enough cash to be able to pick up a gallon of milk weekly. If you don't already have powdered milk, this isn't the time to buy it. It tends to be a lot more expensive than fresh milk.

Milk with lower fat can be frozen. Be sure to remove at least one cup of milk from your gallon jug to allow room for expansion. This works best with skim milk. Any milk with fat will need to be shaken each time you use it.

Grab cheese by the block for the least expensive option. Because we really enjoy cheese, I pick up 2 large blocks for a month. I cut each one in half and package them up separately. I freeze 3 and keep one in the fridge. Remember, cheese is *a condiment* during difficult times, not a main course. You simply cannot afford cheese and crackers for dinner.

Grains

I know this is a wildly unpopular ingredient these days, with all the low-carb and keto diets out there, but grains are the great stretchers of your pantry. You can take one serving of leftover chili and feed your entire family with it when you mix it with rice and a little bit of cheese.

Buy your grains in the biggest packages possible for the most savings. Forget about "instant" anything – these items are often totally stripped of nutrition, and again – you are spending time, or you are spending money. Here are some of the grains to look for:

- Brown rice
- Pasta
- Oats
- Quinoa
- Barley
- Flour
- Cornmeal

There are lots of other grains, but these are inexpensive, versatile, and easy to work with.

Basics

To turn your raw ingredients into meals, you'll need a few scratch cooking basics, too.

- Baking soda
- Baking powder
- Yeast (if you are going to bake bread)
- Spices
- Sugar, Syrup, Honey
- Fats (Cooking oil, shortening, butter, lard, etc.)
- Vinegar
- Salt and pepper

How much should you buy?

This is the tricky part. How much to buy has a lot of variables, and only you can identify them.

- What do you have on hand?
- How big is your family?
- How hungry is your family?
- How picky is your family?

- How long do you expect the budget to be tight?

The best option is to do some meal planning before you go shopping, which we'll talk about next. This should help you identify how much you need for your main meals. Don't forget to add extra for lunches and snacks!

Create a meal plan and a list (but in pencil, not pen)

Before you go grocery shopping, do a quick inventory of what you have on hand. Some important things to note are:

- What do you have that will go bad if you don't eat it right away?
- What almost-meals do you have the ingredients for?
- Are there any special occasions or schedule conflicts during the week ahead?

Plan some meals around existing ingredients, particularly those ingredients that don't have too many days of shelf-life left. Next, if there's a birthday that week, or a sleepover for your kids, what special meal will you serve? What ingredients do you need for that? And finally, are there any days coming up during which you'll need shortcuts, snacks-on-the-go, or something else unusual?

Once you've incorporated these factors, then check your local flyers (those are more often online now instead of stuffed into your mailbox.) Are there any really awesome sales? I'm talking about loss-leader-level sales where you get a ham for 50 cents. (I wish.) If there are some great deals to be had, work them into your menu.

Once your menu is done, make a list of the things you need to make it happen. Are there any outrageously expensive ingredients that you're out of that you only use for this one thing? Maybe reconsider that meal, then.

With the list in hand, you're ready to shop.

Consider once-a-month shopping

I have cut my grocery bills in half by shopping once a month. If you're really focused on cutting costs, this might help you too.

What would happen if you only went shopping once a month? Would you become more organized? Would you become more creative? Would you become more mindful of waste? Would you save a ton of money?

Here's how we do it.

The "Rules"

You can change these around to fit your family's needs, of course, but following you can find our family's guidelines for Once-a-Month Shopping.

- **We take one trip for each of our needs: groceries, animal supplies, and other supplies.** These may all be undertaken on the same day, or they can be split up based on the way your family gets paid.
- **Spend some time checking out the sales at various stores in your area.** We make a day of it, hitting several different grocery stores after checking the sale flyers online.
- **Supplies that can be obtained outside of regular retail environments are exempt.** For example, if you barter with a neighbor, purchase some craft supplies at a yard sale, or go get a bushel of apples directly from a local farmer, these things don't count as "going to the store." This is a way you can make up for a shortfall in your supplies while still abiding by the "no stores" rule. However, ordering a new item from Amazon or another online retailer would be considered cheating.
- **We go out for two meals per month.** This might be

Chinese takeout, pizza delivery, or a restaurant meal. A meal out can break up the monotony and help you stick to your no-stores challenge. Based on your budget and your family's habits, decide if, and how many, meals you'll have out.

- **Don't hesitate to break the rules if it's a matter of health or safety.** Obviously, I don't want to see your dog starve for a week because you underestimated the amount of dog food that you required for the month. Nor would I want someone to go without safety goggles at a new job until the end of the month. Adhere to the no-stores rule only if it makes sense.

If you have health reasons that require you to eat more fresh food, then by all means, work in a second shopping trip each month to pick up those items. When my daughter was dieting, she required some extra veggies to munch on, so we made a second trip two weeks into the month to supply those needs. You might consider other options like sprouting or windowsill gardening in the winter or a full-on vegetable garden in the summer.

Always use common sense with these changes.

How to get started

Plan a trip to each type of store that you use. If money is a problem, you can split these shopping trips up.

- A trip to the grocery store
- A trip to a general merchandise store like Target or Wal-Mart
- A trip to the feed store/pet store if it's necessary for your family

With each trip, you're going to predict what you need to run your household for an entire month. The next article will go into more detail about these shopping trips.

The financial benefits

As prices go up, it's easy to spend a little here and spend a little there until you are shocked to discover that you have nothing left. The easiest way to prevent that might be to stay away from temptation. Going to do your shopping only one time in a month will help you stay away from those impulse purchases that always seem to hop into the cart. It will be easier to keep track of your spending if it's all in one large trip.

When we lived in the city, we got into the habit of "just stopping to get one thing" several times per week. This added up, and our grocery bill got out of control.

When you set yourself a monthly budget, it can be difficult to keep track if you run to the store all the time. But when you shop once a month, you can withdraw the cash you need to purchase your items and stay within your budget more easily.

When I did this before, it made a massive difference in my grocery budget, and I think you'll see the same results. After the first month, it's far easier to shop this way because the money will be readily available when you haven't shopped for several weeks.

The organizational benefits

If you know you only have one shot at getting all your supplies for the month, you're going to be far more organized about that shopping trip.

You'll be forced to calculate your needs in advance so that you can get everything you'll require. You'll need to consider things like special events that are coming up during the month (are you celebrating any birthdays or holidays?), guests that may be arriving, and outings for the kids that might require snacks or certain supplies.

During the month, you can keep a list as you discover things you'd normally "run to the store" to pick up. This list can be fulfilled during the next monthly shopping trip, at which time you may discover that you already found a satisfactory substitute for the missing product.

We also found that when we shopped with an eye toward longer-term groceries, we added to our stockpile without even trying. There were always shelf-stable or frozen food items left at the end of the month that could be put toward our general pantry.

The creative benefits

When you shop on a monthly basis, you'll find that there are many ways to skin a theoretical cat. (Don't skin a real cat. I like cats. A lot.)

If you run out of an item during the month, it's time to put on your problem-solving hat and come up with a replacement that doesn't come from the store. Maybe you can repurpose something you already have. Maybe you can create the item out of supplies you have on hand. Maybe you can find it at a yard sale, borrow it from a friend, barter for it, or simply live without it. Whatever way you find around the missing item, it's sure to get your wheels turning.

16 things you need to know about once-a-month shopping

Prepare to save a lot of money! Here are some tips to help you get started. Soon you'll adapt this way of shopping and make it your own.

Make a menu plan before you go shopping. Even if you veer from the plan, you'll still have the ingredients on hand to make full meals. I like to plan out five dinners per week and leave the other two (plus lunches) open for leftovers. I can cheerfully eat the same thing for breakfast every day, so that's very easy to calculate.

When planning, think about what the ingredients are. Plan to have meals with the freshest ingredients first, then the longer-lasting ingredients, then the shelf-stable or freezer ingredients. Examples below.

Week 1: Foods that are quick to spoil, like salad greens, asparagus, green beans, broccoli, peppers, fresh berries, bananas, zucchini

Week 2: Hardier produce like carrots, brussels sprouts, pears, oranges, cabbage, leeks

Weeks 3 & 4: Now's the time to switch to frozen fruits and vegetables. (You can also use canned or dehydrated. We absolutely love applesauce, for example, and that works well as our week-4 fruit.) Some things that will last well into the fourth week if properly stored are carrots, potatoes, winter squash, turnips, rutabagas, apples, and sweet potatoes.

Head to the store. With these guidelines in mind, when you go to the grocery store, pick up enough fresh fruits and veggies to get you through a couple of weeks. Then, be sure that you have enough frozen, canned, or dehydrated products to see you through the last two weeks.

Pick up enough dairy products for the month. If you have the space, you can easily freeze milk to be used later. The higher the percentage of milk fat, the more you may need to shake it up after it thaws. Cheese freezes well, but you should expect it to crumble instead of slicing when it thaws.

Sour cream tips. It can be frozen if you are planning to use it in baking or cooking but isn't very good if you intend to use it as a condiment. Instead of sour cream, try homemade plain yogurt. It tastes very similar and is quite simple to make yourself. (We'll talk about how to make yogurt later on.)

Eggs will be fine for an entire month in the refrigerator. Think about how many eggs your family eats and stock up. If you don't have enough refrigerator space, then you can freeze one egg per square in an ice cube tray, then move them into a freezer bag when they've frozen solid.

Keep your storage spaces in mind when you're on your shopping trip. Both of our freezers have a bit of space after last month, and there's some room in the fridge, but you want to be careful not to get more than you can cram in. Opt for shelf-stable options if you don't have enough fridge and freezer space.

Think about fresh greens. Start working on those solutions for fresh greens when you can't go to the store: sprouting, a windowsill garden, a greenhouse, a hoop house.

Think ahead about your month. Do you have any special occasions to prepare for? Any birthdays or school parties or potlucks or guests? You'll want to have the right supplies on hand for any unusual events.

It's not just about food. Next, move on to things like toilet paper, laundry soap, dishwasher detergent, and bleach for the month. Keep supplies on hand to make your own if you run out. (Better yet, start off with the supplies and make your own to save money!)

Remember health and beauty aids. Don't forget about personal hygiene items like toothpaste, toothbrushes, shampoo, deodorant, and female supplies. Better to get a bit too much than not enough!

Get supplies for furry, finned, and feathered friends. How much do your pets and livestock need to get through the month in good health? Pick that up at the store and stash it away.

Grab OTC meds. Do you have things like over-the-counter medications and special foods in case someone is under the weather? It's best to stock up on these things ahead of time instead of waiting until you need them. Trust me, as a single mom, when I'm the one who is sick, it's horrible to have to go to the store to pick up medication or ginger ale.

You'll probably have some hiccups, but this will save you all sorts of money in the long run.

Guerilla shopping

What's guerilla shopping? Think of it like guerilla warfare, which is battles waged by combatants who aren't part of the official military or police force. They wage small-scale attacks against conventional forces using more primitive tactics and less advanced weaponry.

Guerilla shopping is using less popular shopping strategies that some folks wouldn't necessarily engage in.

Some folks dumpster dive (Hey, I've done it when I was dirt poor.) Grocery stores often throw out food still in the packages because it's beyond the best-by date. Make sure this is legal where you live. "Daisy told me to do it" won't work as a defense if you get arrested.

You can also make friends with your store's produce manager, deli manager, and butcher. I used to get stuff "for my livestock" all the time, absolutely free. While some of it was only fit for livestock, there was often plenty of salvageable stuff for us if I took care of it right away.

Others shop the last-day-of-sale rack. This is probably the easiest and most common form of guerilla shopping, so I'll talk a bit more about that.

These days, if I can score cheap groceries, I'm practically jumping for joy in the middle of the Piggly Wiggly. (People stare when you do that. #AskMeHowIKnow)

Where are these elusive "cheap groceries," you ask? They're in the humble "last day of sale" aisle. These marked-down foods can be the Frugalite's best friend.

But...they come with a caveat. **You have to manage them *immediately*, or you risk wasting all the money you just spent on them.**

Last week, I went to the store on a Thursday afternoon. I got four prime rib burgers from the meat counter for $1.50. I got a bag of organic lemons as well as a head of sad-looking-but-still-edible cauliflower for a buck each. I got 3 pounds of mushrooms for $2. I also got some pre-chopped sweet potato and diced onion for less than a dollar. Everything got immediately used or put back so that it wouldn't go bad.

Here are some ways to make the most out of last-day-of-sale groceries.

Make dinner from them

First things first, make yourself a yummy dinner with the deals you just got. I usually use the nicest cut of meat and make something delicious with it. Everyone thinks it's a treat, and they have no idea you just basically stole it. I used my prime rib burgers and mushrooms to make tasty burgers with sauteed mushrooms and gravy. I added some mashed potatoes and roasted veggies, and I was a dinner-time she-ro.

You can also make a meal you aren't going to eat right away just to get things cooked up ASAP. Make a soup or stew with your last day of sale goodies and then store it in the freezer to pull out on a busy day.

Roast those veggies

There isn't much I love more than roasted vegetables. Cut away anything that looks less than appetizing. I like to toss them in olive oil, season them with my homemade seasoning salt, and drizzle them with a teeny tiny bit of honey.

I use roasted veggies in lots of different ways. First, there are just plain old roasted veggies – they're a wonderful side. But I use them after that too. You can reheat them in the oven for the best texture, or you can use them cold in salads.

From my recent grocery expedition, I roasted those sweet potatoes along with some garlic, onion, and cauliflower. I had them the night I went shopping, and then I used the leftovers for a tasty "bowl." I love, love, love veggie and chicken bowls. This one had brown rice, roasted veggies, and diced chicken, and I drizzled the entire thing with Thai peanut dressing. Absolutely divine.

You can also puree your roasted veggies for a decadent and flavorful soup.

Bake something

Did you end up with a crap-ton of bananas or zucchini? Whip out the baking supplies and make yourself some tasty bread. You can eat them right away or let them cool, then stick them straight into the freezer for later. I've also made a memorable impromptu pie from a bag of iffy pears and a carton of berries.

Freeze stuff

A lot of things are fine to go straight into the freezer. I stash away any last-day-of-sale meat that I'm not cooking that day straight into the freezer. Make sure the packaging is still okay – you might need to rewrap it with plastic wrap or a big ziplock. It would be a shame to bring it home and save it, only to end up throwing it out later due to freezer burn.

Some produce can also go into the freezer. I used the little snack zipper top bags to divvy up my diced onion. Most herbs can go straight into the freezer, and fruit for smoothies or baking can, too.

Dehydrate things

My dehydrator has been humming along non-stop since my trip to the store, dealing with all those mushrooms and the lemons. I'll add the lemons to herbal tea blends. I powdered the lemon peel and the mushrooms for tasty seasonings. (They don't take up much space this way, but you still get the nutritional oomph from it.)

Other things that dehydrate well are fruits, greens, root vegetable slices, and peppers. Did you know that you can also dehydrate bread? Yep, you sure can. Add your own seasonings to it and stash it away for your own stuffing mix, or zap it in the food processor to make your own panko-style bread crumbs.

Can it

If you enjoy canning, consider using this method for putting back some of your goodies. I've made pressure canned soup, and I've water-bath canned homemade jams and apple sauce from the last day of sale aisle.

The last-day-of-sale can be the best day of your week if you do it right.

Okay...let's get cooking!

Basic Batches

Yo! Where my basic batches at?

Oh...over here?

Before we get started, let's talk about some basic scratch-cooking foods and techniques that will save you a bloody blue fortune. I'll give you as many options as possible for each of them, because i don't want you to feel like you need to rush out and buy new appliances and stuff.

How to cook rice

One of the thriftiest additions to stretch a meal (or to use as the basis of one) is the ever-so-humble rice. It's a primary ingredient in exotic cuisines around the world, from Latin America to Europe to Asia. Depending on how you spice it up, it can be a tasty addition to a wide variety of entrees.

Even with the rampant inflation that we're experiencing right now, you can still get a pound of white rice for approximately 92 cents and brown rice for about $2.75.

For reference, you can get 7-8 one-cup servings per pound of rice. That's a lot of rice bang for your rice buck!

Some people find rice to be challenging to get just right. If that's you, look no further. The solutions to your rice-making problems are here! These recipes are for the regular, cheap white rice you get in big bags at the store.

How to cook rice on the stovetop

Rice on the stovetop requires a teeny bit of attention, and this is where people often go wrong. I know that I have forgotten I had rice on the stove before, and the resulting smoke in the kitchen when it burned to the bottom of my pot was less than pleasant.

Here's how you do it.

- 2 cups of white rice
- 3 cups of water

Bring your rice to a boil on the stovetop, then reduce it to a simmer. Put a lid on and set your timer for 13 minutes. Remove the rice from the heat, leave the lid on, and let it sit for 10-15 minutes. Fluff it with a fork and serve.

How to cook rice in the oven

This is my all-time favorite way to cook rice. I do this when I'm baking or roasting something else in the oven, even if I'm not serving rice with that particular meal. It's completely hands-off.

- 2 cups of white rice
- 3 cups of water

Bring your water to a boil on the stovetop. Meanwhile, put rice into an oven-safe dish that is big enough to hold the water. Stir the boiling water into your rice, put the lid on your dish (or cover it with foil if you don't have a lid for your dish), and pop it in the oven at 350F for 30 minutes. (Note: After you've done this a couple of times, you'll be more comfortable baking it at different temperatures to go along with whatever you're baking.) When your thirty minutes are up, pull the dish from the oven and let it sit, covered, for 10-15 minutes before serving.

How to cook rice in the crockpot

This is another completely hands-off way to cook rice. It does take longer, but if you're planning ahead, you can pop it into the slow cooker and forget about it until dinnertime.

- 2 cups of rice
- 4 cups of water

Either spray the inside of your pot with nonstick spray or rub it with butter or cooking oil. Otherwise, your rice WILL stick. (Ask me how I know.) Add your rice and water, then cook it on high for about 2 hours. Give it a stir at the two-hour mark and taste-test it to make sure it's tender. If not, give it another half hour, adding water if needed.

How to cook rice in the microwave

Once, when we were about to move, we didn't want to drop a thousand dollars to refill our propane tank. That meant we went three weeks without a working stove. My daughter cooked rice in the microwave during that time. It's easy but not any quicker than the stovetop method.

- 1 cup of rice
- 2 cups of water

Bring your water to a boil in the kettle or use the microwave. Add the boiling water to a microwave-safe bowl and stir in the rice. Microwave it on high for 12 minutes with no lid, then top it with a lid and let it sit for 10-15 minutes before serving.

Variations: The fun part of cooking rice

Now we get to the fun part – variations on basic rice. Below are several different ways to jazz up your rice.

1. Toast the rice in cooking oil on the stovetop before cooking it.
2. Switch out beef, chicken, or vegetable broth for the water.
3. Add half a bag of frozen mixed vegetables at the end of your cooking time.
4. Season it with your favorite spice blend.
5. Add a bouillon cube to the cooking liquid.
6. Switch out the cooking liquid for coconut milk.
7. Add garlic powder and parsley.
8. Stir in some butter.
9. Top it with finely shredded cheese.
10. Indian Rice: Cook it with a cinnamon stick, 4-6 cloves, and some garlic powder. Remove the cinnamon and cloves before serving.

How to stretch a meal with rice

Here are some ways you can use cooked rice to stretch a meal.

1. Replace pasta with rice for a thrifty twist on saucy meals.
2. Serve leftover chili on a bed of rice to make it go further.
3. Make fried rice with protein leftovers, veggies, and a couple of eggs.
4. Stir it into a small serving of soup to turn it into a casserole.
5. Add milk, fruit, cinnamon, nutmeg, and honey to make a tasty breakfast porridge.
6. Top it with leftover gravy.
7. Add cooked beans and spice it up with your favorite flavors.
8. Add it to the filling of stuffed peppers or cabbage rolls.
9. Prep protein bowls with rice as a base.
10. Add tomato sauce and Mexican seasonings.

How to cook beans

When most people think about the cheapest, relatively nutritious food around, they think of beans and rice. A lot of folks stock up on canned beans, certain that dry beans are too much hassle and too time-consuming. But learning to cook dry beans from scratch can save you a ton of money if beans are a regular part of your diet. The

National Bean Institute reported you could save more than $80 a year if you're a once-weekly bean-eater by making them from scratch instead of buying them canned.

Not only are you saving money, but if you are worried about sodium intake, you can completely control it when you cook beans from scratch at home.

As a born-and-raised Southerner, I've often turned my nose up at canned beans. The home-cooked version is just so much tastier and has a far better texture. Here's everything I know about how to cook dried beans.

Sorting and soaking

You can't just dump beans from their plastic bag straight into your cooking pot. They have to be sorted and soaked first. If you skip these two steps, you're likely to run into problems like weird rocks in your beans, bad flavors, and/or extremely long cooking times.

First, let's talk about sorting. I always rinse my beans in a big colander before putting them in the pot to soak. Then, I simply relocate the beans 1-3 at a time into the pot. I'm looking for several different things I don't want to include in my pot. First, I'm checking for beans that have gone bad – these can be identified easily because they're wrinkled, small, shriveled, and discolored. Some have bug holes in them.

Secondly, I'm looking for things that don't belong: twigs, tiny pebbles, even the occasional bug. You may think this is gross, but trust me, you are checking your beans far more carefully than the beans that ended up in your can from a factory.

Once I have my beans in the pot, it's time to soak them. I generally soak them overnight, but using this method does have them ready to go in about 4 hours. Don't be dismayed by this prep time – 95% of it is hands-off.

Add 8 cups of water to every two cups of dried beans. Approximately 2 cups of dried beans are equivalent to 1 can of prepared beans. I usually cook about 4 cups of dried beans and use the leftovers in recipes.

Place your pot on the stove and bring it to a hard boil for about 2 minutes. Put the lid on and remove it from the heat. Then, just leave it there until morning.

I like to drain my beans and use fresh water for cooking. This removes some of the starches that make beans difficult to digest for some folks. However, you don't have to do that if you don't want to. You can cook them in the soaking liquid if water is scarce.

How to cook beans on the stovetop

To cook your beans on the stove, replace the soaking water and cover them by at least two inches with fresh water. Bring your beans to a simmer, but not a hard boil. This keeps them from splitting open.

Cook your beans for 2-4 hours on a low simmer. Stir the beans frequently to make sure they don't stick, and be sure to add water as needed.

Add non-acidic seasonings at any point in time. If you have anything acidic to add, wait until the last half hour, as this can prevent the beans from getting tender. I also wait about half an hour before they're done to add table salt. If I'm cooking them with some kind of meat (bacon, hambone, or something else), I put that in from the beginning. I also add onions early on if I'm using them.

How to cook beans in the crockpot

This is the easiest thing in the world.

Put the beans in the crockpot. Cover them with about two inches of water. Add your seasonings. Cook on low for about 4 hours.

How do you know the beans are ready?

I use the taste test. Take one out, let it cool off, and bite into it. I prefer my beans to be quite tender, but everyone has a different preference. That being said, be sure there isn't too much hardness to it, or it will be unpleasant to eat a serving of them. As well, it should be noted that some beans, when undercooked, can make you ill.

How to cook grits

Looking for a tasty, versatile, and inexpensive side dish? Look no further than a humble bag of grits. The ways to eat grits are countless, but we'll start with 10 simple and frugal ones here.

Growing up in the South, grits were a staple of our diet. I'll never forget shortly after I got married, going grocery shopping in Canada and searching fruitlessly for grits. My inquiries of the store employees were met with blank stares, and I thought to myself, "They must be called something different here."

When my husband got home from work, I said, "You won't believe it, but I went to two different stores today and couldn't find any grits."

He gave me the same blank, puzzled stare as the grocery store workers and asked me the words that will ring in my ears and make me giggle forevermore. "What's a grit?"

While my fellow Southerners are laughing, let me give you the lowdown on grits. Grits are a very coarsely ground dried corn product cooked into something similar to porridge or other hot cereal grain. I don't know too many people who are ambivalent about grits. You love them or you hate them. If you hate them, I would suggest that you may have had them poorly prepared and cooked with water. If you can get your hands on some at a good price, try one or more of the following ways to eat grits and you may find yourself a pro-grits convert. They're a great addition to your Cheap Eats repertoire.

Shopping for grits

The main difference between grits and polenta is simply the color of the corn. Grits are typically made from white corn, and polenta is made from yellow corn. Polenta is a bit more coarsely ground than grits, and a bit fussier and more hands-on to cook. However, anything you can do with grits, you can do with polenta, and vice versa. Just get whichever is cheapest – or if you're not in the South, whatever is available.

For the love of Jack Daniels, don't get those little packets of instant grits. They are cooked, then dried out, and then recooked, and it sucks out the flavor and nutrients. Cooking grits from scratch is not difficult and makes a world of difference in your end product.

For corn products, I always select organic ones if possible. I personally prefer to avoid GMOs when I can, but if that doesn't bother you, conventional will cook up the same way.

Grits 101: How to cook them

Grits are as easy to cook as rice – seriously. For nearly any recipe you're going to make with grits, you'll start with this simple base.

Ingredients:

- **4 parts liquid:** I use half milk and half water. Non-dairy oat milk works fine for this. Depending on your final recipe, you might wish to use broth in place of milk for a savory dish. You can also cook your grits in water and add some milk or cream at the end.
- **1 part dry grits:** I prefer stone-ground, but "old-fashioned" grits have a longer shelf life and cook

faster.

- **1/2 tsp–1 tsp of salt**: Even if you are making a sweet dish, your grits need a little salt.

Directions:

1. In a saucepan, bring your liquid to a boil.
2. Add your salt.
3. Slowly stir your dry grits into the boiling liquid.
4. Cover it and reduce it to low heat.
5. Simmer the concoction for 15 minutes for old-fashioned grits and 45-60 minutes for stone-ground grits, stirring occasionally. Because I'm forgetful, I set a timer for every 5 minutes to remind me to stir.

You'll know your grits are ready when they've reached a gloriously cream consistency. Take a spoonful out, let it cool enough not to burn your tongue, and taste a tiny bit to make sure the grits are soft without crunchy pieces. If there are still crunchy pieces, you may need to add a bit of hot water and cook it for longer.

You can also make basic grits in the crockpot or the instant pot if you prefer to be more hands-off.

Now that your grits are cooked, how will you serve them? If you're going to make them into any type of cake or patty, you need to spread them out and let them chill in the fridge for an hour or so. Otherwise, carry on seasoning your grits.

Ways to eat grits

There are so many different ways to eat grits I'm just scratching the surface. Once you've fully embraced your love of grits, the sky's the limit.

Buttered grits

Buttered grits are the easiest way to serve them. You can use this as a side dish for breakfast, lunch, or dinner. Simply stir in a hefty helping of butter and some black pepper once your grits are cooked. When I have leftover buttered grits, I stir in a little milk to thin them down before heating them up, and then I serve them in place of mashed potatoes or rice as the base for other foods.

Cheese Grits

Cheese grits are utterly glorious and versatile. You can use any kind of cheese. Our particular favorites are extra sharp cheddar and Parmesan. When your grits are done cooking, add anywhere from half a cup to a cup of cheese to your steaming hot pot of grits. I often season cheese grits with onion powder and black pepper.

Shrimp and grits

This is the Southern classic that Forrest Gump made mainstream. I'm not personally a fan of crustaceans, but the book would not be complete without this – one of the most popular ways to eat grits.

While your grits are cooking, fry up a couple of slices of bacon in a skillet. Put your cooked bacon to the side. Then add peeled, deveined shrimp, garlic, chopped onion, and Cajun seasoning to your bacon grease and fry it up until your shrimp turns pink.

You can add cheese to your grits if you want, although it's not part of the classic recipe. Top your grits with the shrimp mixture, then crumble up your reserved bacon (you didn't eat it while you were cooking, did you?) on top of that.

The base of a breakfast bowl

You can make a fabulous savory breakfast bowl by topping buttered grits with bacon or sausage, some sauteed onions and peppers, and a fried egg.

Grits and gravy

If you don't have any biscuits kicking around or don't want to turn on the oven to bake them, make white gravy from sausage or bacon and ladle that on top of your hot grits.

Grits casserole

There are SO MANY casseroles based on grits. My favorite is made with sausage. While your grits are cooking, fry up your favorite sausage – I prefer crumbled breakfast sausage – along with onions and peppers. When all this stuff is cooked, then beat some eggs in a large mixing bowl. Scramble them lightly in your sausage pan. Grease a casserole dish. Stir in all your ingredients and some cheese until everything is well combined. Bake this divine concoction at 350F for half an hour.

Sweet grits

Another way to eat a bowl of grits is to season it up like oatmeal. Add stuff like brown sugar, maple syrup, chopped pecans or almonds, fruit, cinnamon, nutmeg, or granola, and enjoy.

Parmesan grits cakes

After cooking your grits, immediately stir in some Parmesan cheese, garlic powder, onion powder, black pepper, and salt. Spread the mixture out in a pan and put it in the fridge for an hour to chill.

Heat your favorite cooking oil on the stovetop. Cut little squares of the chilled grits concoction and fry them for 3 minutes on each side. Let them drain on a paper towel.

You can serve this with a marinara dip or as a base for an Italian dish like chicken cacciatore or chicken Marsala.

Thanksgiving grits

Do you make cornbread dressing for Thanksgiving? You can skip the step of making cornbread and just use cooked grits instead. Dressing is not stuffing. It is cooked aside from your turkey. I cook my grits in chicken broth for this recipe. Cook your grits a day ahead of time and leave them in the fridge. About an hour before the turkey is done, stir in a couple of raw eggs, sage, salt, black pepper, onions, mushrooms, and any other delightful additions you put in dressing. Pop this into a greased baking dish and cook it in the oven at 325 for approximately an hour or until it's firm and slightly crisp on top.

Fried grits

This could not possibly be about a Southern food without instructions for frying it. You can make your fried grits sweet or savory. I'll give you the basic instructions and then some variations.

Spread them out in a pan and let your cooked grits cool for at least an hour, but preferably overnight in the refrigerator. Next, you're going to batter them. Beat a couple of eggs in one dish, and put some seasoned flour in another. Cut your wedges of chilled grits, and dip them first into the egg wash, then into the flour. Plop that right in a preheated frying pan with your cooking oil of choice while you continue making wedges of grits. Fry them for about 5 minutes per side. Then put them on a paper towel to drain a little of that grease from your fried grits.

Variations:

- Add salt and pepper to the flour and serve them as a side dish to eggs and bacon. (An alternative to hash brown potatoes)
- Top them with butter and maple syrup, and eat them like pancakes.
- Add the savory seasonings of your choice to the flour. Top your fried grits with leftover Cajun food like gumbo or jambalaya.

The sky is the limit with fried grits!

How to make gravy

Maybe it's because I grew up in the South, but to me, nothing helps stretch a meal, pull things together, or disguise less-than-stellar quality food like gravy. You can put gravy on just about anything, and suddenly, the meal feels far more hearty.

I make two basic kinds of gravy – brown gravy and white gravy.

Both are pretty similar to start out with. You are going to brown some flour in some fat. It's what you add next that changes things. For brown gravy, broth is the gold standard for a rich, savory gravy. However, if times are tight, water, salt, and pepper can make a fine gravy as well. For white gravy, you'll be adding milk, salt, and pepper for a creamy, flavorful sauce. In difficult times, I usually use water and a couple of tablespoons of powdered milk for my white gravy. (Keep reading – the specific recipes are below.)

How to make brown gravy

This is how to make a simple brown gravy.

Ingredients

- 2 tbsp of meat drippings
- 3 tbsp of flour
- Salt and pepper to taste
- 2 cups of broth, drippings, or water

Directions

1. Add drippings to a saucepan and turn the heat on your stove to medium.
2. When the drippings are hot enough that a tiny bit of water splashed into the skillet off your fingertips

sizzles on contact, use a whisk to mix in 2 Tbsp of flour. Whisk vigorously until the flour and fat are completely incorporated with no lumps. You should end up with a smooth, creamy-looking mixture. (This is called a roux.)

3. Stir in the water or broth. Broth gives a slightly richer flavor, but gravy made with water is still delicious and much more frugal. Using the whisk, mix the roux and water thoroughly.

4. Cook, whisking almost continuously, for 3-5 minutes until your gravy reaches a uniform consistency and the desired thickness. If it is too thick, whisk in more liquid, half a cup at a time.

5. Keep warm over the lowest heat your stove allows.

Gravy *rocks* because it can make a lesser cut of meat taste delicious. Your gravy leftovers (if you have any) can be used as the basis of a nice soup or stew.

How to make white gravy

The directions for white gravy are almost identical to making brown gravy.

Ingredients

- 2 tbsp of meat drippings
- 3 tbsp of flour
- Salt and pepper to taste
- 2 cups of milk or 2 cups of water and 4 tbsp of powdered milk or 1 cup of water and 1 cup of milk

Directions

1. Add drippings to a saucepan and turn the heat on your stove to medium.
2. When the drippings are hot enough that a tiny bit of water splashed into the skillet off your fingertips sizzles on contact, use a whisk to mix in 2 tbsp of flour. Whisk vigorously until the flour and fat are completely incorporated with no lumps. You should end up with a smooth, creamy-looking mixture. (This is called a roux.)
3. If you are using milk powder, whisk that into your roux.
4. Stir in the milk or water. Using the whisk, mix the roux and milk or water thoroughly.
5. Cook, whisking almost continuously, for 3-5 minutes until your gravy reaches a uniform consistency and the desired thickness. If it is too thick, whisk in more liquid, half a cup at a time.

6. Keep warm over the lowest heat your stove allows.

I really think gravy is the best frugal condiment around. It makes even the plainest meal more savory and filling.

How can you use gravy?

Gravy goes with just about anything at our home. But here are a few specific ideas.

Brown Gravy:

- Simmer hamburger patties or cube steaks in brown gravy and serve over mashed potatoes or rice. You can add some sauteed onions, mushrooms, and/or peppers to this dish to extend it inexpensively. This can also be cooked in the crockpot.
- Top French fries with brown gravy. If you want to be Canadian, add cheese curds before you add the gravy (or shredded cheddar).
- Make your roast go further by making gravy from the drippings or cooking liquid.
- Meatballs and gravy are delicious served over noodles.
- I always make brown gravy with the drippings from a roasted chicken and drizzle it over everything on my

plate.
- Meatloaf is lovely with gravy.

White Gravy:

- The eternal Southern classic: biscuits and gravy – use a small amount of bacon or sausage to get your drippings, then crumble the meat into the gravy at serving time.
- Chicken-fried steak with white gravy.
- Shredded chicken in white gravy (you can either top it with biscuit dough or serve it over potatoes).
- Pork chops – if you make shake-and-bake style pork chops from a thinner cut of meat, white gravy will make the meal more filling (and tastier).
- Fried chicken with mashed potatoes and white gravy is another Deep South classic.

Any gravy:

- Add gravy to vegetables and leftover meat, then put it inside a pot pie.
- Add gravy to leftover meat, vegetables, and grains, then thin the gravy with broth or water to make a leftover stew. Serve with bread.
- Bread and gravy: my Dad grew up during the Great

Depression. For him, a favorite meal was a slice of bread (from a store-bought loaf) drenched in any kind of gravy. (This is a good way to use up leftover gravy – I read some people actually have leftover gravy!)

Fry bread

It's always important to have a quick bread in your frugal repertoire, and this one, with its roots in Native American tradition, fits the bill. The first time I had it, it was used for tacos, so you can find the filling recipe below.

Ingredients:

- 1 ½ cups of flour
- 1 tsp of salt
- 1 tbsp of shortening
- ½ tbsp of baking powder
- ¾ cup of water
- Cooking oil or shortening for frying

Directions:

1. Mix all the ingredients together with half a cup of the water and knead until you have a nice soft dough.
2. You may need to add extra water to get a nice dough.
3. Let it rise on the counter for 15 minutes.
4. Add cooking oil or shortening to a skillet and heat it up until it sizzles when you flick a drop of water on it.
5. Then, pull off small pieces of dough, roll them into little balls, and then flatten them into circles.
6. Drop them into the skillet and fry them for about 2-3 minutes per side.
7. Use a slotted spoon to transfer them to a plate lined with a paper towel.

You can use this as a fast side-dish-food-stretcher or as a yummy taco shell.

Ingredients (Filling)

- I pound of ground beef
- 1 can of pinto beans, drained
- 1 tsp cooking oil
- 1 tbsp chili powder

- 1 tbsp cumin
- 1 tsp onion powder
- 1 tsp garlic powder
- ¼ cup of ketchup
- Salt to taste

Directions for the filling

1. Heat some cooking oil in a skillet, then add the beef crumbles and lightly brown them.
2. Stir in the beans and seasonings and let it cook for about 10 minutes.
3. Add the ketchup (I know it sounds weird, but trust me) and cook for another 5 minutes.
4. Put this aside while you make the fry bread.

Assemble the tacos

1. Scoop a spoonful of filling onto each piece of fry bread.
2. Dress up your tacos with any fresh vegetables you might have, and consider some cheese, hot sauce, sour cream, and salsa.

Fry bread is a fast and useful side dish to serve with all sorts of soups and stews – you get all the goodness of homemade bread without having to wait for yeast bread to rise and bake.

How to make biscuits

Another multi-purpose recipe, you can use this to make biscuits or a biscuit-dough topping.

Ingredients:

- 2 cups of flour
- 3 tsp of baking powder
- 1 tsp of salt
- 1 tsp of sugar
- 1/2 cup of milk
- 1 tbsp of white vinegar
- 3 tbsp of cooking oil

Directions:

1. Preheat oven to 425F.
2. Mix milk and vinegar in a small bowl and allow it to sit for about 5 minutes.
3. Mix flour, baking powder, sugar, and salt in a bowl. Add milk and vinegar mixture, and oil.
4. Stir just enough to hold the dough together.
5. Knead lightly about 10 times on a well-floured

surface.

6. Pat or roll dough about 1/2-inch thick.
7. You can move the dough in one piece over to your pie pan or you can cut circles with a floured drinking glass and place the individual biscuits on the dish you are topping.
8. Bake for 15-20 minutes or until golden brown. Top with butter if desired.

This recipe can be used for biscuits – simply bake for 10-15 minutes.

As well, you can roll this dough out and cut it into thin strips, dropping it into boiling broth until it floats to the top (7-10 minutes) to make dumplings.

How to make pie crust

The beauty of my granny's pie crust recipe is its versatility – you can use what you have. Ideally, I use butter and water for the fat and liquid. However, I have used many different ingredients with excellent results. This recipe makes enough for one double-crust pie or two single-crust pies.

Ingredients:

- 3 cups of flour
- 1 cup of fat (butter, shortening, coconut oil, lard, vegetable oil)
- 2 tsp of salt
- ½ cup of liquid (water, milk, whey)

Directions:

1. Place your liquid in a dish with a few pieces of ice, if available. Keep this in the refrigerator while you're combining the other ingredients.
2. Combine the flour and salt.
3. Cut the butter or fat into tiny pieces and incorporate it into the flour mixture, either with a pastry cutter, a food processor, or a couple of knives. Once the mixture resembles cottage cheese curds, you have combined it sufficiently.
4. Add your ice water to the mixture a couple of tablespoons at a time. This is where practice makes perfect – after you make this a couple of times, you will begin to know when it looks and feels "right". Use a fork to mix this into the dough – if you use your hands, you will heat up the dough too much, and the crust won't be as flaky.
5. You don't want to dough to be wet and sticky – you

want it to be sort of stringy and lumpy. When you think you have the right consistency, squeeze some dough in your hand – if it stays into a nice firm ball, it's time to move on to the next step. If it is crumbly and doesn't stick together, you need more water.

6. Make the dough into two balls and press them down. Place them, covered, in the refrigerator for at least an hour.

7. On a floured surface, roll out the dough with a heavy rolling pin until it is thin but not broken. Fold your circle of dough into quarters and carefully move the dough over to your pie pan.

Bake as per your recipe's directions or at about 375F for approximately 45 minutes for a two-crust pie or 35 minutes for a one-crust pie.

Two super easy ways to make homemade yogurt

Yogurt is full of good bacteria, and it's delicious, too! But those little six-packs touting "active cultures" are also filled with other ingredients that you probably don't want to add to your diet if the purpose of eating yogurt is good health.

Homemade yogurt is super frugal

It gets even better. Not only is homemade yogurt healthier than store-bought, but it's also much less expensive, particularly if you prefer to give your family organic or raw dairy products.

Here's the math:

A gallon of milk makes approximately 2 quarts of yogurt.

- 1 gallon of organic milk is $6.99 from our local Safeway.
- 1 quart of organic yogurt is $4.99.
- By making our own yogurt, using a little of a previous batch to start the new batch, the cost per quart is only $3.50.

It's very easy to make

It's easy to make yogurt at home. The only issue for some folks is that it is time-consuming. While it does take time, it isn't all hands-on time. You have to be near the stove to watch the temperature of the milk. Because of this, I usually start my milk as we're finishing up dinner, then finish the process as I'm cleaning up the kitchen for the day. Since I'm going to be in the kitchen for an hour then anyway, it doesn't seem like I'm spending a huge amount of time making yogurt.

There are cool little yogurt-making machines that you can buy for a very reasonable price – less than $30. But you don't have to have a machine to make yogurt. I'm going to tell you about two very simple methods for making yogurt. You can go off-grid and make it in a thermos, or for larger batches, you can use your dehydrator.

The first steps are the same for both methods. (Actually, the first steps are the same if you have a yogurt-making machine too.)

How to make homemade yogurt

Definitely DO try this at home.

Here's what you need:

- 1/2 gallon of milk (2 quarts)
- Culture: 1/4-1/2 cup of organic full-fat yogurt OR 2 packets of freeze-dried starter
- Food thermometer (I prefer a digital instant-read)

That's it...

Directions:

- In a large saucepan, gently bring the milk up to 165 degrees Fahrenheit. Some people, when using raw milk, raise the temperature only to 120 so that they don't pasteurize the milk. (However, when you turn the milk into yogurt, you'll be adding in healthy bacteria, so this is entirely optional.)
- When your milk reaches the desired temperature, remove it from the heat and allow it to cool. Be sure to remove it from the element if you have an electric stove or it will continue to get hotter. If you go over 185 degrees, your yogurt may not turn out well.
- Allow your milk to cool to anywhere between 108 degrees and 112 degrees. If it is any hotter than that when you mix it with the culture, you'll kill the bacteria that turn the milk into yogurt. If it is cooler, then it won't be warm enough for the culturing process to occur. (This specificity is why I recommend a digital instant-read thermometer.)
- When the milk drops to the desired temperature, ladle out about a cup of it to mix in another bowl with your culture. (This can be yogurt from the store, yogurt from a previous batch, or freeze-dried starter.) Whisk it *gently* to combine it thoroughly.

Gently. You're not making whipped cream or meringue.

- Pour the mixture back into the pot with the rest of the milk and whisk gently to combine it well.

This is where the paths of yogurt-making part, but read all the way to the end, because the paths merge again.

How to make yogurt in a thermos

This is an off-grid way to make yogurt. It's useful because adds to the lifespan of your milk if the power goes out. I generally use this method because it uses no power, and I like to be thrifty. Use a good quality, large thermos for this. Don't use one of those little-kid, plastic lunch box thermoses. A thermos is a good thing to have around for the Cheap Life, so you'll find this to be a multipurpose item.

- While you're prepping your yogurt, fill your thermos with hot water so that the temperature inside it is nice and warm when you pour in the mixture. If the mixture cools down too quickly from meeting the chilled walls of the thermos, your yogurt will not turn out.
- Empty the thermos, reserving the water for some other use.

- Pour or ladle the mixture from the pot into the thermos. Use a funnel to help guide the milk into the thermos. (Scroll down to the end of the article if you want a giggle about this.)
- Put the lid on the thermos immediately.
- Leave the thermos in the warmest place in the house overnight. For us, this is the laundry room at our current home. At another home, we tucked the thermos behind the wood stove.
- Allow your yogurt to culture in the thermos for 10-14 hours. The longer you leave it, the more tart it will be.
- (You're not quite done. Be sure to skip down to the "Last Steps" section.)

How to make yogurt in a dehydrator

This method can be used if you have one of those nice large dehydrators with removable trays like the Excalibur . It must have removable trays and temperature settings for this to work. If you are going out and buying a dehydrator specifically for the purpose of making yogurt, it would be much better to get the yogurt-making machine instead. And by better, I mean $200 cheaper. However, if you already have an Excalibur or similar dehydrator, this is just one more use for it.

- Heat up enough Mason jars to hold all of the milk you're preparing by filling them with hot water and setting the lids on top of them.
- Remove the shelves from your dehydrator and begin preheating it to 105 degrees.
- When your milk has been mixed with the culture, empty the water from the jars.
- Using a canning funnel, fill the jars with the yogurt-to-be, leaving an inch of headspace.
- Place the lid on the jars. (I use old lids that have previously been canned with for this, since I don't need a seal.)
- Place the jars in your dehydrator and close it. Leave the temperature at 105 degrees and allow the jars to stay in for 10-12 hours. (Some instructions say 8 hours, but my yogurt was watery when I did that.) The longer the yogurt stays in the warmth, the more tart it will be.

You're not quite done...read on.

Last steps

When you make homemade yogurt, it isn't immediately going to have the super-thick texture that you get with store-bought yogurt.

Some people stir in a thickener like unflavored gelatin. When you do this, you have the goodness of the whey and you don't have to take the extra steps of draining it.

However, I prefer to drain my yogurt and use the whey for other purposes.

- Place a large colander in a larger bowl.
- Line the colander with a lint-free, clean dish towel.
- Pour the yogurt into your draining setup. It will be very liquidy but don't despair!
- Drain the yogurt for at least two hours. The longer you drain it, of course, the thicker the yogurt will be. I like to pull mine when it is the texture of sour cream, but if you leave it overnight, it will be the delicious thick consistency of cream cheese.

You'll have lots of whey left over from this process. This can be used for lacto-fermentation, in place of water or milk in baking, in smoothies, or to make ricotta cheese. (Stay tuned for a ricotta recipe!) If you have livestock, they also love whey.

Just so you know...

You know how websites always make things look easy and flawless? That is the magic of Bloggerland, and I think sometimes it can be discouraging for those who are trying new things.

Well, just so you know that all is not actually perfect in Bloggerland, I poured from the pot to the thermos this time and used a funnel with a narrow neck. I overflowed the thermos, and milk went everywhere, to the point that I had to pull out the stove and clean the floor beside, under, and behind it. I just wanted you to know that we all try experiments that don't work or make enormous messes from time to time. ●

8 delicious ways to eat yogurt

If you don't eat yogurt on a daily basis, you might be shortchanging your health. There's no easier way to get some healthy bacteria in your system than to enjoy some rich, delicious, full-fat yogurt loaded with active cultures.

If your gut is damaged, a daily dose of yogurt can actually repair the damage. Not only that, but a good quality yogurt can:

- Help to prevent gastrointestinal infections
- Help your body fight off food poisoning or stomach viruses
- Boost your immune system

- Prevent osteoporosis
- Reduce acid reflux

Often, people who suffer from lactose intolerance are absolutely fine with consuming yogurt, because the live cultures break down the difficult-to-digest lactose.

Not just any yogurt will do

Don't just run to the store and grab those little 6 packs of yogurt and feel nutritionally saintly, however. Despite the health claims, the flavored conventional yogurts are the absolute opposite of health food. If you're purchasing your yogurt, opt for the full-fat variety for the maximum dose of delicious nutrients.

The best option of all is homemade yogurt, which is surprisingly easy to make. When you make it yourself, you control the type of milk used (we make ours from raw milk) and can flavor it as desired with fresh fruit, honey, real vanilla, herbs, or organic sugar.

Making your own is so easy, I'm not sure why everyone doesn't do it.

Savory or sweet, there's a yogurt idea out there for everyone!

1. **Yogurt cheese:** Line a mesh strainer with a coffee filter. Place this on top of a bowl. Place your yogurt on top of the filter. Put this in the fridge and allow it to drain overnight. You'll be left with a rich thick substance. You can eat this as "Greek yogurt" or as a substitute for cream cheese, spreading it on bread and bagels.

2. **Yogurt dip:** Use a thicker yogurt and season it any way you would generally season sour cream to make a dip for veggies. We especially like it with a little garlic powder, salt, and loads of finely chopped dill. (You can use dried dill from your spice cabinet if fresh is unavailable.)

3. **Yogurt "sour cream":** Thick yogurt can be used in place of sour cream. Instead of merely adding fat with few nutrients, you can add a big pile of creamy vitamins to the top of your baked potato. You can also use yogurt in place of sour cream in recipes like stroganoff or curry.

4. **Yogurt salad dressing:** You can make "ranch" dressing with the addition of some onion powder, garlic powder, dill weed, salt, and pepper.

5. **Yogurt smoothies:** Mix yogurt with frozen fruit and zip it in the blender for a tasty and nutritious shake. Some people like to add sugar or honey to this, and depending on your nutritional needs, you can also add a scoop of a healthy (not artificially sweetened) protein powder. This is a great use for a batch of

homemade yogurt that turned out runny.

6. **Yogurt parfaits:** Mix a drop of vanilla extract and a touch of sugar to plain yogurt. (You can stir in some vanilla protein powder for something rich and pudding-like.) Then top it with fruit and crunchy granola. Delicious and satisfying.

7. **In baking:** Yogurt can be used as an egg substitute when baking. You can use 1/4 cup of yogurt in place of each egg that the recipe calls for.

8. **Yogurt "ice cream":** Use a ratio of 1:1 yogurt and frozen fruit. Sweeten according to taste. Puree in the blender, then place in the freezer for an hour. If your resulting creation is too hard to eat with a spoon, pop it back in the blender for about 30 seconds.

Yogurt is an amazing staple that belongs in every kitchen!

How to make homemade pasta without eggs

Easy homemade pasta without eggs can be yours – and very inexpensively! This can be a fun family project if you have kids, too. And the taste? There is absolutely no comparison to that dry stuff in the box!

My recipe is egg-free because one of my daughters was allergic to eggs when she was younger. I came up with this when I needed a nice wide "egg noodle" type pasta for a recipe. Even after she outgrew the allergy, we kept the recipe because it was so delicious. This is made from 100% shelf-stable and basic ingredients.

Please note that this isn't really a time saver and only saves a little bit of money. But it's a fun project, and it tastes delicious.

Ingredients:

- 3 cups of flour
- 1 cup of warm water
- 2 tbsp of olive oil
- 1 tsp of salt

Optional: Spices of choice, up to 2 tbsp in total (garlic powder, onion powder, spinach powder, rosemary, basil...the sky is the limit!) You can also use vegetable powders to change the color of the pasta.

Directions:

1. Place your flour in a large mixing bowl and stir in the salt (and any other dried spices you have opted

to put in).

2. Make a well in the center and pour in the water and olive oil.

3. Gently incorporate the ingredients with a fork. The best way to do this is to push a little bit of the flour mixture at a time into the liquid, then add a bit more of the flour mixture, and keep doing this until it is all well incorporated.

4. Knead the mixture for about 10 minutes and then let it rest for half an hour, covered with a damp towel. When you come back to it, the dough should feel soft and silky under your fingers.

5. Knead and let it rest for another half hour.

6. Roll out the dough with a rolling pin, then cut it with a sharp knife, or use a crank pasta machine. You can cook it immediately or let it sit, uncovered, for half an hour. (I like to let it sit before cooking – I think it holds its shape better!)

7. Depending on the thickness of your pasta, cook it in boiling water or broth from 1-2 minutes. Don't overcook it, or it will turn into mush.

It really is that easy to make homemade pasta without eggs.

If you want to get fancier, there are loads of good books solely about the art of pasta-making, and if you are making it on a regular basis, life will be much easier with a pasta maker.

Simple spice blends that are cheaper to make than buy

If you're anything like me, you absolutely love a well-seasoned dish of food. But spice blends are super expensive! Just one ounce of taco seasoning in a little packet costs a dollar. You can make your own for a fraction of the price, and you can control what goes in it. You can limit the salt and sugar if you want, or even omit it. You can avoid chemical concoctions like monosodium glutamate and simply combine delicious, healthy spices and herbs to create your own delicious concoctions.

Here are some of the simple spice blends that I always keep on hand.

Taco seasoning

I love, love, love Mexican food and make it at least once a week. Here's my personal blend of delicious spices.

- 4 tbsp chili powder
- 1 tbsp cumin
- 1 tbsp onion powder
- 1 tbsp garlic powder
- 1 tsp black pepper

- 1 tsp oregano

Optional:

- 1 tsp brown sugar
- 2 tsp Salt
- 1/2-2 tsp cayenne pepper

Add salt and cayenne pepper to taste. Cayenne can really turn up the heat!

Burger seasoning

Do you have a favorite burger seasoning? Mine is pretty simple, but my family loves it.

- 2 tbsp onion powder
- 1 tbsp garlic powder
- 1 tbsp smoked paprika
- 1 tsp black pepper
- 1 tsp mustard powder

Optional

- 1 tsp salt
- 1/2 tsp white sugar

Italian seasoning

Use this seasoning to jazz up meatballs, chicken, or your favorite Italian soup or sauce.

- 4 tbsp basil
- 3 tbsp oregano
- 2 tbsp thyme
- 1 tbsp onion powder
- 1 tbsp garlic powder
- 1 tsp sage
- 1 tsp smoked paprika
- 1/2 tsp chili powder (trust me)

Optional

- 1 tsp salt

Greek seasoning

I love this seasoning on grilled chicken, in meatballs, and sprinkled over a greek salad or a hunk of feta cheese.

- 3 tbsp oregano
- 2 tbsp parsley
- 1 tbsp dried lemon zest
- 1 tbsp garlic powder

- 1 tsp rubbed dill weed
- 1 tsp black pepper

Optional

- 1 tsp salt

Season-anything salt

This is my own knock-off of my beloved Lawry's Season-All.

- 2 tbsp salt
- 1 tbsp paprika
- 2 tsp white sugar
- 1 tsp onion powder
- 1 tsp garlic powder
- 1 tsp chili powder
- 1/4 tsp ground turmeric
- 1/4 tsp celery salt

If you're watching your sodium, you can dial the salt down – that's the joy of making your own seasoning blends!

Salt-free seasoning blend

This is basically a DIY version of Mrs. Dash. You can remove anything you or your family dislikes when you make your own.

- 3 tbsp garlic powder
- 1 tbsp basil
- 1 tbsp marjoram
- 1 tbsp thyme
- 1 tbsp parsley
- 1 tbsp onion powder
- 1 tbsp sage
- 1 tbsp ground black pepper
- 1 tbsp dried lemon zest
- 1 tsp cayenne pepper
- 1 tsp cumin

Optional:

- 1 tsp savory
- 1/2 tsp mustard powder

New Bay

If you're a fan of Old Bay seasonings for your Bloody Marys and seafood, you can make a very similar version of your own using the following:

- 2 tbsp celery salt
- 2 tsp paprika
- 1 tsp mustard powder
- 1 tsp ginger
- 5 bay leaves
- 1/2 tsp black pepper
- 1/8 tsp nutmeg
- 1/8 tsp mace
- 1/8 tsp allspice
- 1/8 tsp cinnamon

Ragin' Cajun

Maybe it's the Southern gal in me, but I absolutely love Cajun food. A lot of it is made with inexpensive base ingredients and then beautifully spiced with a seasoning mixture that will get your mouth tingling.

- 2 tbsp smoked paprika
- 1 tbsp dried oregano
- 1 tbsp black pepper

- 1 tbsp onion powder
- 1 tbsp garlic powder
- 1 tsp dried thyme
- 1 tsp dried basil
- 1-2 tsp cayenne pepper

Optional:

- 2 tsp salt
- 1 tsp sugar

This is so so so delicious in red beans and rice!

Poultry seasoning

Sprinkle this seasoning generously on your chicken before baking, or mix it into your batter before frying. It's also tasty on your holiday turkey!

- 3 tbsp sage
- 2 tbsp thyme
- 1 tbsp onion powder
- 1 tbsp garlic powder
- 1 tbsp black pepper
- 1 tbsp dried lemon zest
- 1/4 tsp nutmeg

Optional:

- 1 tsp salt
- 1 tsp white sugar
- 1 tsp marjoram

Bulk spices to keep on hand

You can combine the following bulk spices to create almost all of the above with just a few small additions that you probably already have in your spice cabinet. I keep my bulk spices in completely dry mason jars for longevity and freshness.

- Chili powder
- Oregano
- Basil
- Garlic powder
- Onion powder
- Salt
- Sugar
- Smoked paprika
- Cumin powder
- Cayenne pepper
- Lemon peel powder
- Thyme

In smaller quantities, I also keep on hand:

- Sage
- Marjoram
- Dill weed
- Dry mustard
- Mace
- Allspice
- Nutmeg
- Cinnamon

With these spices, I can create many different meals. My family loves a variety of foods from around the globe, and these basics are prevalent in many different cuisines, allowing me to capture a multitude of flavors. When you're on a budget, it's important to be able to create variety with the same old basic ingredients, and seasoning is a wonderful, thrifty way to do so.

Be sure to check out any local ethnic grocery stores for bulk spices, as well as the ethnic food aisle in your grocery store.

How to make your own Everything Bagel Seasoning

On a recent road trip, I spent an astonishing amount of money at Starbucks buying a little plastic box with fruit, a muesli pita bread, boiled eggs, and peanut butter. I was unprepared for an extra day on the road and grabbed the healthiest-looking thing I could find and gritted my teeth all the way to the cash register.

But in this box, I discovered something magical.

There was a teeny, tiny packet of Everything Bagel seasoning tucked under the eggs.

I had never even considered putting that on boiled eggs, but it was absolutely delicious. I started thinking about what else I could put that seasoning on.

I looked up the seasoning and found that Trader Joe's has a popular one called Everything But the Bagel seasoning. And then I saw it was $8.49 for a jar of it. And of course, then I thought of how I should make the seasoning for myself. The ingredients are super easy to find at most grocery stores, and you may already have most of the items on hand. Once you buy them, you can make numerous batches of Everything Bagel seasoning. (Maybe even for a homemade gift?)

Everything Bagel Seasoning recipe

This delicious seasoning has only five ingredients and will add some flavorful crunch to just about anything.

- 2 tbsp poppy seeds
- 2 tbsp sesame seeds
- 1 tbsp minced garlic (dried)
- 1 tbsp minced onion (dried)
- 1 tsp coarsely ground sea salt (you can add more salt if this isn't enough)

Actually, I hesitate even to call this a recipe.

You put all this stuff into a little jar, shake it, and you're done.

What can you flavor with Everything Bagel Seasoning?

Here are just a few things that could be made tastier with your new seasoning mix.

1. Boiled eggs
2. Cream cheese on a regular bagel
3. Avocado toast
4. Garden-fresh sliced tomatoes

5. Potato dishes
6. Chicken
7. Fish
8. Noodles with butter
9. Egg, tuna, or chicken salad
10. Macaroni salad
11. Potato salad
12. Coleslaw
13. Garden salad
14. Popcorn
15. Grilled cheese sandwiches

The sky's the limit. You can use this to add some savory crunch to just about anything!

FrugaliTEA: How to make your own herbal tea blends

Do you enjoy a steaming cup of herbal tea? It's one of the simple pleasures that I most enjoy. I like the entire ritual of it. Putting the water on to boil. Placing sweet local honey in a beautiful mug. Loading up my infuser with fragrant herbs. The sound my spoon makes when it rings against the mug, and I stir everything together.

I noticed the last time I was at the store that the price had gone up on herbal tea bags. (Of course, the price has gone up on just about everything.) Not that this is enough to make or break you, but tea bags ranged from 20 cents apiece to 40 cents apiece, depending upon the brand.

There's a far better and cheaper way to make herbal tea, my dear Frugalites. Make your own! For a small investment up front, you can buy organic herbs by the pound on Amazon or at many different online retailers. As well, I dehydrate the herbs I grow, as well as random citrus peels and other elements of herbal tea, for even thriftier ingredients. There are a few things I often grab in tincture format, especially if I don't use them every day.

Then, all you need is a tea ball or an infusing mug, and you're paying single-digit pennies per cup. What's more, your blends are personalized and probably a lot higher quality than the ones you get at the store.

How do you use loose tea?

There are all sorts of ways to use loose tea. In fact, you can find entire websites dedicated to the art. I like to keep things simple, though, and also thrifty.

I own a mug with an infuser insert and lid. It's not fancy, but it matches my black and white dishes, and it is one of the more reasonably priced options.

I also like tea strainers. They're a little bit bigger than those tea balls with the squeezy opening mechanism, and I find them far easier to fill.

Making tea this way is simple. Fill your tea strainer or infuser with about two tablespoons of loose herbs and pop it into your mug. Add your honey if you're using it. Boil your water and pour it over the infuser. Pop a lid on it (you can also use a saucer) and allow it to steep for 5-15 minutes. Remove the infuser or strainer, give it a stir, and enjoy your super-thrifty cup of herbal tea.

Below are some of my favorite blends

These are just suggestions for blends. Make them your own according to your likes and dislikes (and what you have on hand). Play around with the ratios until it tastes right to you.

Get-'Er-Done Tea

Got stuff to do, but your get-up-and-go got up and went? Try this get-'er-done tea for a boost of herbal energy.

- Lemon Peel
- Orange Peel
- Ginseng
- Green Tea

Peace Tea

Have you had a stressful day? Are you feeling anxious? Do you need to wind down and chill out? Peace Tea is a blend containing calming herbs that may support relaxation.

- Lemon Balm
- Peppermint
- Chamomile
- Skullcap

Feel-Better Tea

Are you feeling under the weather? Depending on what ails you, this tea can help with its fragrant herbs and medicinal properties. I always make this when someone is suffering from a cold or flu. The slippery elm bark helps soothe a cough, and I prefer to use a few drops of tincture instead of the dried material. If you don't have slippery elm, you'll still find the tea beneficial.

- Peppermint

- Slippery elm
- Chamomile
- Elderberry
- Orange peel
- Hibiscus flower

Tummy-Ache Tea

Looking to settle your stomach? This combination can help support digestion and calm an upset stomach. If you are vomiting or have heartburn, leave out the ginger. Slippery elm tincture is my go-to for heartburn.

- Peppermint
- Chamomile
- Ginger
- Slippery elm

Sweet Dreams Tea

One of the most popular teas out there is Sleepytime Tea by Celestial Seasons. And for good reason – the ingredients are gentle and pleasant in taste. You can make your own version with these herbs.

- Chamomile
- Peppermint

- Lemon verbena or Lemon balm
- Passionflower
- Skullcap
- Hibiscus flower

Courage Tea

Nearly everyone has seen the movie *Practical Magic*, with Nicole Kidman and Sandra Bullock. But did you know that it's based on a delightful four-book series by Alice Hoffman? These books will transport you to a quaint, charming home by the sea, where magic abounds and whimsical lore is a part of everyday life. In the books, the Owens women make a drink called "courage tea" whenever someone needs a boost. Because my daughters and I love both the books and the movie, I concocted a tasty blend inspired by the tea that sustained generations of the fictional family. It's really tasty, and perhaps it'll make you feel braver.

- Ginger
- Lemon peel
- Orange peel
- Elderberry
- Red rooibos
- Star anise
- Black pepper

Recommended ingredients for herbal tea blends

Here are some of the things that I always keep on hand for tea blends. Most herbs I get by the pound, but smaller packages are available. It would be a big expense to get everything at once. Start small and add to your tea-ingredient collection on a monthly basis.

- Peppermint
- Chamomile
- Lemon and orange peel (I dehydrate my own from fruit I eat or use in cooking, and then zap it in the food processor)
- Hibiscus flower
- Elderberries
- Slippery Elm (dry or tincture)
- Passionflower
- Skullcap (dry or tincture)
- Lemon balm

PS: Homemade herbal tea blends and an infuser would make a lovely holiday gift basket that won't cost much if you use bulk herbs you purchased for yourself anyway.

Ultimate Frugal Formulas

On my website, TheFrugalite.com, I love to make "The Ultimate Frugal X Formula." It's a recipe that isn't a recipe – in fact, it's more like a math problem or a science project.

2 (carbs) + 1 (creamy thing) + 1 (protein) + 1 (veggie) = result topped with 1 (crunchy thing)

And really, isn't cooking just science anyway?

This chapter will contain some of my Ultimate Frugal Formulas and serves as a good basis for the rest of the book.

The Ultimate Frugal Casserole Formula

I know, I know. Casseroles sound very "50s Housewife."

But when you're on a budget, casseroles are a great way to make a little bit of food stretch further in a tasty way. I often use leftovers that aren't enough to feed the whole family as an ingredient in a delicious, thrifty casserole.

And, to make it even better, there's a formula.

Here's the formula

This is inspired by and loosely based on Amy Dacyczyn's Universal Casserole recipe from *The Complete Tightwad Gazette*.

- 1 cup of protein
- 1-2 cups of veggies
- 1-2 cups of carbs
- 1 1/2 cups of sauce
- Spices
- Topping

It's honestly that easy.

Your protein might be leftover meat, a can of tuna, ground meat, lentils, or beans.

Your veggie can be any tasty thing you have that will go well with the meat. You can use either frozen or canned green peas, green beans, cauliflower, broccoli, or mixed vegetables, just to name a few.

Your carbs can be pasta, rice, potatoes, or whatever grain you have kicking around in abundance.

Your sauce is the "glue" that holds the whole thing together. It might be white sauce, gravy, a can of condensed cream of whatever soup, tomato sauce, or cheese sauce.

Casseroles are pretty yummy when they have some kind of **tasty, crispy topping**. This might be bread crumbs and butter, cracker crumbs and butter, shredded cheese, those little cans of French-fried onions – whatever tasty thing you have on hand.

Season it with whatever **spices** you have that are appropriate – Italian seasonings, garlic salt, chili powder – whatever you think sounds good with your concoction.

How to make a casserole

To make your casserole, combine your cooked meat, your frozen or canned veggies, your cooked carbs, your spices, and your sauce.

Bake at 350 for 30-45 minutes, or until your sauce is bubbling. Then add your topping and bake it for another 5-10 minutes until it is crispy.

And that's it

Seriously...how easy are casseroles?

The Ultimate Frugal Soup Formula

One of the best ways to stretch a meal is by taking a small amount of food and creating the ultimate frugal soup! You don't even really need specific ingredients for this. You can use the guidelines in my Ultimate Frugal Soup recipe and assemble that strange mish-mash in your fridge into a delicious and satisfying meal.

Not only is soup thrifty in good times, but it can make things much better during bad times. It's warm, comforting, and can go a looooooong way to feed many mouths.

You need liquid, protein, produce, starches, and seasoning for a nicely balanced bowl of soup. (Below, I'll talk more about each of these.)

The nice thing about Ultimate Frugal Soup, however, is that you can use what you have on hand. The only absolute necessities are liquid (because, um...it's soup) and at least one other ingredient.

Ultimate Frugal Soup is a great way to use up leftovers and combine the things you have on hand into something tasty and filling. If you add bread, you can stretch it even further.

I often use the crockpot for Ultimate Frugal Soup. At night, when I'm putting away leftovers, I like to combine complementary items into the crock, put the lid on, and pop it into the fridge. A couple of days later, when I have enough veggies and meat in the crock, I will add my liquid and cook it on low all day. It's so nice to arrive home to the delicious smell of soup.

Liquid

The sky is the limit when it comes to the liquid you're going to use for your soup. Think about your other ingredients when choosing a liquid, and be sure that it will combine nicely. Whatever liquid you use, you can go with a minimum of a 50:50 ratio of liquid and water to make a less expensive yet still rich-tasting soup.

Here are some ideas for liquids you can use.

- Tomato juice
- Crushed tomatoes
- Broth (beef, chicken, vegetable, etc.)
- Vegetable puree

If you don't have any of these things on hand, you can start your liquid the night before. Simply put 10 cups of water in your crockpot and add onions, garlic, celery, and/or a whole carrot. Season it with a little bit of salt. Cook it on low overnight, and you'll have a tasty golden broth to which you can add your other ingredients the next day.

Another choice is to use beef, vegetable, or chicken bouillon in water. I don't like to consume MSG, so I usually go with an organic bouillon or one that is MSG and gluten-free.

I add the liquid last. I put in all the other ingredients and then top off my crockpot with my chosen liquid and water.

A Few Options

If you want a creamy soup, cook it with a broth base. Then about two hours before serving time if you are slow-cooking and 15 minutes before if you are stovetop cooking, you can make it creamy. You have a few different options.

- Add a cup of milk or cream. (For a non-dairy option, cashew milk is a nice addition.)
- Puree a large cooked potato or a can of white beans

and stir in the puree.

- Add one cup of sour cream or plain Greek yogurt if it's something that will go with the flavor of the soup.
- Scoop out a cup of the soup liquid into a bowl and then thicken it with cornstarch, flour, or arrowroot starch. Get all the lumps out in the bowl, then pour it back into the soup and stir well.

Liquid is the base of your soup, and your choices are really important to the end result.

Protein

If you want to make a meal that will stick to your ribs, you need protein in your soup. I often use leftovers for my protein. Here are some ideas for protein-rich additions for Universal Soup.

- Beef
- Chicken
- Pork
- Sausage
- Ham
- Pinto beans
- Kidney beans
- Navy beans

- Lentils

If you are using meat, it can be a variety of different textures: diced, ground, or shredded. If you are using legumes in your soup, you will either need to use canned beans/peas or presoak them the day before.

I like to use 1/2 a cup of protein per person. But if the situation is not ideal and you are cobbling together leftovers, just use what you have.

Produce

Soup is a great way to do two things: use up random leftover veggies and get more produce into your family. Don't worry if your leftover vegetables have butter or other seasonings on them – this will just add to the flavor of the soup.

Depending on how you are cooking your soup (quickly on the stovetop or slowly in the crockpot), this will affect your decision on what kind of produce to add and when to add it. If you are doing a quick stovetop soup, add everything at once. If you are slowly cooking your soup, follow these guidelines:

- **Leftover vegetables**: Add them in the last hour of cooking. If you put them in all day, they'll be mushy and unpleasant at serving time.

- **Canned vegetables**: Add them when you start the soup and use the liquid they're canned in for your base liquid. I find this one of the very best uses for canned veggies.
- **Frozen vegetables**: Add them in the last 2 hours of cooking – they're pre-cooked and don't need much time.
- **Fresh vegetables:** Starchy vegetables like turnips or carrots take longer to cook. You should dice them into small pieces to make certain they'll be cooked thoroughly and put them in at the beginning of your cooking time. Other more delicate vegetables like peas, corn, summer squash, broccoli, and green beans only need a few minutes, so I suggest putting them into the crockpot during the last half hour.

You can use whatever produce you have kicking around. I often put together a nice soup with one can each of peas and carrots, corn, green beans, potatoes, and diced tomatoes. I use all the juices and then add ground beef (raw if you are crock-potting all day, cooked if you are doing a fast stovetop soup.) This is a soup so easy that even a non-cook can make it.

Starches

Starches extend your soup and turn it into a filling meal. Here are some great starches, along with when to put them in. With most starches (other than potatoes), I prefer to cook them separately and stir them in toward the end. They soak up a lot of liquid, particularly rice. But worst case scenario, if it is cooked in the crockpot all day, you will end up with something more casserole-y than soup-y. An exception to this is pasta – definitely do not add it at the beginning of the day and hope for the best. You will not get "the best."

Potatoes – Is it even soup if there are no potatoes? They should be put in at the beginning, regardless of whether you are cooking in a crockpot or cooking on the stovetop. Dice them into small, bite-sized pieces.

Pasta – Don't put the pasta in too early or you will have a bowl of mush. Look at the package and double the time required. So if the package says the pasta will take 10 minutes to cook, put it in about 20 minutes before serving time. Be sure to taste a piece to make sure that it is thoroughly cooked.

Rice – I often cook rice in a separate container because it soaks up so much cooking liquid. I really think that is the best way to go about adding rice to soup. Add your cooked rice about half an hour before serving time to allow it to absorb flavors without absorbing all your broth.

Barley – My favorite barley is pearl barley. Before cooking barley, you should rinse it and pick through like you would with beans. Add the barley at the beginning of cooking time and go with about 2/3 of a cup – it gets much bigger when it cooks. Watch your liquid to see if you need to add more about an hour before serving time. If you're cooking it on the stovetop, barley needs about 45 minutes.

Bulgur – This is some yummy stuff derived from wheat berries (so beware if you are gluten-free), and a lot of vegetarian recipes use it as a substitute for ground beef due to the slightly similar texture. Some prep work is needed for bulgur. Put it in a large, heatproof bowl and pour boiling water over it. Allow it to soak for about 15 minutes, then drain it before adding it to your recipe. Bulgur can go into the crockpot in the morning or takes about 25 minutes on the stovetop.

Farro – Farro should be rinsed before adding it to your soup. One cup of farro will be sufficient for an entire pot. Put it in at the beginning of your cooking time and watch to see if you need to add more liquid.

There are all sorts of other grains you can add. Consider millet, sorghum, amaranth, freekeh, wild rice...so many different grains. If you are using something unfamiliar, I urge you to cook it separately until you learn the ins-and-outs of that particular grain. If you can't tolerate gluten, don't be afraid to sub in a gluten-free grain for your recipe.

Seasoning

Soup can be seasoned any way you want, but below you'll find a few ideas. The measurements are up to you – some folks only want mild flavor while others want intense flavor, and it also depends on how much soup you're making. So I'm listing off spices, and it's up to you to assemble it how you want. Add salt and pepper to taste on all these.

- Tomato-based soup: Basil, oregano, garlic, onion, parsley, marjoram, and thyme.
- Mexican or Southwestern: Chili powder, cumin, onion, garlic, smoked paprika.
- Chicken broth-based soup: Sage, oregano, garlic, onion, parsley, and thyme
- Creamy soup: Thyme and just a teeny tiny dash of nutmeg
- Beef broth-based soup: Thyme, paprika, garlic, onion, oregano, and parsley

Obviously, use what you like and skip what you don't. You will never see rosemary in one of my soups, but if you love it, go for it! A lot of people have particular spices they really dislike. For example, some folks think that cilantro tastes like soap while other people absolutely adore it. (This is genetic, interestingly enough.) Different spices can really help the same-old, same-old taste brand new, so don't be afraid to experiment.

The Ultimate Frugal Muffin Recipe

Here's another addition from the Book of Amy, to which I've added a few of my own twists. You can make muffins out of just about anything if you follow this guideline.

- 2 to 2 1/2 cups grain
- 1 cup liquid
- Up to 1/4 cup fat
- 1 egg (or egg substitute)
- Up to 1/2 cup sweetener
- 2 teaspoons baking powder
- 1/2 teaspoon salt
- Up to 1 1/2 cups additions
- 1-2 teaspoons of spices

Let's take a closer look.

Grains

Use white flour for at least half of the grain. Then you can add all sorts of tasty things for the rest – it could be all flour, whole wheat flour, cornmeal, oatmeal, crushed breakfast cereal, spelt flour, or chickpea flour. But the fun doesn't stop there. You can also use cooked whole grains, easy peasy. Reduce the liquid by 1/2 cup and the dry grain by 1/2 cup. Then, add in a cup of cooked oatmeal, rice, quinoa, or grits.

Liquid

The standard ingredient here is milk. But you can use whatever kind of milk you want: oat milk, soy milk, almond milk, rice milk…you get the idea. As well, you can toy around with the fat content in your milk. Anything from cream to skim milk. (Or make your own "skim" milk by watering down 2% half and half with water.) You can also use fruit juice, buttermilk, or "sour milk." (Sour milk is simply one cup of regular milk to 1 tbsp of white vinegar.

Fat

Say it with me, friends. "Fat is flavor." Don't go making a sad, fat-free muffin. You're broke, not dead. Try lard, cooking oil, coconut oil (my absolute favorite (I get it by the 2-gallon tub), butter, or even nut butter.

Eggs

If you don't want to use eggs, there are all sorts of subs out there to make a tasty dish without the addition of the oval stuff. One of my daughters was allergic to eggs, so I've tried them all. The very best one is one tablespoon of flax seed powder well mixed with one tablespoon of water. You can also use a tablespoon of yogurt or applesauce in place of an egg. We'll talk more about egg substitutes in a later chapter.

Sweetener

Sugar pie, honey bun, you know I looooove you. You can use white sugar, brown sugar, whatever kind of artificial sweetener you prefer, maple syrup, molasses, or honey. If you use a liquid sweetener, cut your dry grain by a quarter cup. This recipe is very versatile – you can go anywhere from 2 tbsp to a half cup of sweetener.

Additions

And here's where it gets fun. What the heck are you putting in your marvelous muffins? Here are a few ideas:

- Berries
- Chopped fruit such as apples or pears
- Nuts
- Seeds
- Shredded carrots or zucchini
- Mashed cooked pumpkin or carrot
- Mashed banana
- Applesauce
- Mashed, drained, canned fruit
- Raisins or craisins
- Shredded coconut

Spices

Choose spices that go well with your other ingredients, such as cinnamon, nutmeg, allspice, a splash of vanilla, clove (just a teeny bit), and/or grated citrus peel.

Savory muffin additions

Cut the sweetener to 2 tablespoons, then go wild with a tasty combo of shredded cheese, finely diced onion, shredded zucchini, Parmesan, diced chili peppers, diced jalapenos, sundried tomatoes, corn, chopped cooked bacon, or diced ham. Season these with parsley, dill, onion powder, garlic powder, or celery salt.

How to make them

1. Grease your muffin tin and preheat your oven to 400.
2. Mix your ingredients until everything is well combined but still lumpy.
3. Plop it into your muffin tin until each cup is about 2/3 filled.
4. Bake for 20-25 minutes, or until a knife you put in comes out clean.

When my daughters were little, I'd make either a cast iron pan full or a muffin pan full of cornbread with blueberries in it. They'd eat it hot from the oven, slathered in butter, and sometimes dipped in maple syrup. It was a thrifty way to get a hot breakfast into them.

The Ultimate Frugal Stir Fry Formula

Never underestimate a stir fry for using up odds and ends in your refrigerator or the goodies you got from the last-day-of-sale rack. Much like soups and casseroles, it's formulaic. Allow me to introduce the Ultimate Frugal Stir-Fry Formula.

I make them 2-3 times per week with a variety of seasonings and sauces, based on the ingredients that I have on hand. The first thing to get out of your head is that stir-fries must be Asian cuisine. While there are many glorious Asian stir-fries, I have several different stir-fry concoctions that are anything but Asian. There's no reason you can't use the appropriate proteins, carbs, and veggies to make a Tex-Mex stir-fry, an Italian stir-fry, or a Greek stir-fry, just to name a few examples.

As with all formulas, some specific components are necessary, but these can be mixed and matched and made to fit what you have on hand. Here are the basic components of the Ultimate Frugal Stir-fry Formula.

- Protein
- Vegetables
- Fat
- Seasoning
- Carb

- Sauce

The key to a good stir fry is cooking all your foods evenly. So, generally speaking, you can't throw in all the ingredients at once, or you will end up with a mix of overcooked and undercooked foods. That is definitely not "ultimate," and you are making an "*ultimate*" stir fry.

One of my favorite guides to stir-frying food is *The Moosewood Cookbook* by Molly Katzen. It's a vegetarian cookbook, but you can throw meat into any of the recipes for the carnivores in your family. It goes into exquisite detail about how to chop things up, what to put in your pan first, and how to ensure even cooking of all your ingredients.

Let's take a closer look at our components.

Protein

Your protein can start out cooked or uncooked, depending on what you have around. If it's starting out uncooked, it will likely be the first thing that goes into your wok or skillet.

- Beef
- Chicken
- Turkey

- Pork
- Shrimp
- Lunchmeat
- Cooked garbanzos
- Canned beans
- Egg, cooked or raw
- Tofu

Those are just a few ideas – remember, this is *your* stir-fry. The Ultimate Frugal Stir-fry Formula is only a guideline.

Vegetables

Again, we're going with what you have on hand. You can use fresh, frozen, or even canned veggies for a stir-fry. The trick to adding canned vegetables is to drain them extremely, extremely well. I let mine sit in a colander while I'm cooking the ingredients that take longer. If you are using canned veggies, throw them in the frying pan when you put in your carb and seasoning. That way, they get browned and have a better texture.

Any veggie can go into a stir-fry. My kids LOVE a stir-fry that I make with sweet potato, broccoli, and chicken.

Fat

You can use a wide variety of different fats for a stir-fry, but try to use something that has a high smoke point. You are going to be cranking up the heat toward the end and you want things browned, not burned. What is a smoke point?

> A cooking oil's smoke point refers to the temperature when the oil starts to smoke—which it will reach before its boiling point. Heating oils past their smoking point has been linked to the formation of carcinogens and can also create an off, burnt flavor. [1]

These are the oils with the highest smoke points:

- Avocado oil
- Canola oil
- Corn oil
- Peanut oil

You may not care for some of these oils due to their GMO origins or potential health issues. The choice of which oil to use is entirely up to you. This is just a guideline.

1. Very Well Fit: https://www.verywellfit.com/smoke-points-of-cooking-oils-4781972

Other fats such as lard, coconut oil, and olive oil can be heated to a fairly high point, but they begin to break down nutritionally.

Seasoning

Onions and garlic are always staples of any stir fry I make, and while they're technically veggies, I put them in the seasoning category.

You can use spice blends to make all kinds of different stir fries. Whether you make the blends yourself or purchase them already made, consider the following for your own Ultimate Frugal Stir Fry Formula.

- Chinese 5-spice
- Thai seasoning
- Garam masala (for curries and Indian flavors)
- Taco seasoning
- Montreal steak spice
- Italian spice blend
- Adobo seasoning
- Greek spice blend

Choose a seasoning that goes well with the ingredients with which you are working. Don't go crazy with the salt because many of the sauce ingredients also contain salt.

And note that a tiny pinch of brown sugar can really bring out the flavors.

Carbs

To make this more filling and stretch the ingredients a bit further, use an inexpensive carbohydrate such as rice or noodles to add to your stir fry. Cook the carb before adding it in.

It goes without saying that if you are on a special diet that requires you to abide to a lower level of carbohydrates, leave this ingredient out or sub in some bean sprouts for a similar texture to noodles.

Sauce

This is another place you can get super creative. Mix and match the following to come up with your own sauces. Make a sauce that goes along with the type of cuisine you've prepared. It would taste pretty weird to add peanut sauce to a Greek stir-fry, right? This is the proverbial icing on the Ultimate Frugal Stir Fry Formula cake.

- Broth

- Soy sauce
- Coconut aminos
- Oyster sauce
- Fish sauce
- Hoison sauce
- Rice wine vinegar
- Apple cider vinegar
- Balsamic vinegar
- Peanut butter
- Cola
- Honey
- Lemon or lime juice
- Fruit juice

The sky really is the limit when making your own sauce. Make it in a separate container, and be sure to taste test it before adding it to your skillet.

How to Use the Ultimate Frugal Stir Fry Formula

Gather up all of the ingredients you've chosen from the lists above (or from your imagination). Now, let's get started using the Ultimate Frugal Stir Fry Formula. Notice that there are no quantities listed. This is a fly-by-the-seat-of-your-pants kind of thing that depends on what you have and how many you're feeding.

- Heat about half of the fat you intend to use in a large skillet or wok on medium heat.
- If you need to cook your meat, add some onion, garlic, and the meat to your skillet and saute it until it's cooked through.
- Remove the meat from the skillet. I like to put mine in a bowl lined with paper towels to catch the excess fat.
- Add in your vegetables. First, cook the ones that take the longest amount of time, like carrots, potatoes, etc. Then add sturdy but faster-cooking veggies like broccoli and cauliflower. Finally, stir in the things that only take a couple of minutes, such as bean sprouts and shredded cabbage.
- This is where the stirring and the frying come into play. Add some more fat and crank the heat up to about 8 on your dial. Stirring constantly, add in your seasoning, carbs, already-cooked meat, and any drained canned veggies. Do this for 3-5 minutes until they are lightly browned or have the texture you desire.
- Next, pour in your sauce. Stir everything well, turn the heat down to 3 or so, pop a lid on it, and let the flavors meld for 3-5 minutes.

Dish it out, and if you want, top it with some fresh herbs, chopped peanuts, crunched-up wontons or tortilla chips, or whatever goes with your flavor sensation.

The Ultimate Frugal Salad Dressing Formula

This is the creation of my daughter, Chloe Morgan.

Homemade salad dressing? For something that is honestly so simple, very few people seem to make it.

Chloe wrote, "Growing up in my home, like many homes, we tended to go for store-bought salad dressings. And why not? It was quick, it was easy, and they tasted good enough. But as I got older, I learned to love my grandmother's homemade salad dressing more and more.

When I was younger, the salad wasn't typically my favorite part of a meal. But when I went over to my grandma's? I loved it. I devoured it. And eventually, I started asking how to make it. That was when my eyes opened to a whole new aspect of cooking that I'd known nothing about before."

The basics of homemade salad dressing

The easiest way to make a homemade salad dressing is simple. A lot of it you kind of play by ear (or is that tongue, since it's by taste?) Everyone is different, so it only makes sense that we like slightly different things. The following are just the basics for your salad dressing, but they can be elaborated, changed, and adjusted based on what you and your family like.

- 2 tbsp oil
- 1 tbsp of something acidic (think vinegar or lemon juice)
- 1/2 tbsp of something sweet.
- Some simple herbs
- Chopped up garlic and/or onion (this can be fresh or dehydrated, and for onion, I especially love using red or green onion.)
- Salt-and-pepper to taste

Mix all your ingredients together, and that's just about it!

Everything listed above can be adjusted. This is just the basic salad dressing formula to start with. From there, you may find that there needs to be a little more vinegar, a little sweeter taste, or even a little more herbs. When all is said and done, though, it is super easy!

If we break into the nitty-gritty of homemade salad dressing, here is what you need to know...

Oils

If possible, use a higher-quality oil, such as avocado oil or olive oil. Some other good ones you can try are pumpkin seed oil (this one is packed full of flavor), liquid coconut oil, or any other high-quality oil.

Acid/Vinegar

Think fancy vinegar. Here are some great ones to use;

- Apple cider vinegar
- Red wine vinegar
- White wine vinegar
- Balsamic vinegar
- Red wine
- Lemon juice
- Lime juice

In a pinch, though, don't be afraid to use plain old cheap white vinegar.

Something sweet

How much you use will kind of depend on what type of sweetness you use. Start with a 1/4-1/2 tablespoon. Use what you have on hand.

- White sugar
- Brown sugar
- Maple syrup
- Honey
- Agave syrup
- Or, if you're feeling very creative, you can try crushing a handful of raspberries for a raspberry vinaigrette.

Herbs

Keep it simple here. Limit it to 1-2 types of herbs. Fresh will give you the best flavor, but dried works just as well! If you are using dried herbs, though, let the dressing sit for about five minutes or more while you get the rest of the salad prepped so the flavors can meld a little more.

Here are some popular salad-dressing herbs.

- Thyme
- Rosemary

- Sage
- Oregano
- Basil
- Parsley

Prefer creamy salad dressings to vinaigrette?

That's no problem at all. This formula is easily customizable into a creamy dressing that will leave your family wanting more.

Instead of using oil, substitute two tablespoons of oil for two tablespoons of heavy cream or one tablespoon of mayo (depending on how thick you want your dressing to be).

Cheap Eats

One of the best ways I've found to stretch the grocery budget is by adding in "Cheap Eats." We had a whole roster of such meals when my daughters were younger. The criteria for "Cheap Eats" was that it had to be reasonably filling, quick to make, (cooking utilities add up, too), and less than a dollar a serving.

Let me preface this with the fact that Cheap Eats aren't necessarily the healthiest of meals, but when your budget is tightened to this level, you can't afford fancy organic crackers made from gluten-free grains ground with volcanic stones under the full moon. So, while you want to be as balanced as you can in order to stay healthy, your healthy diet is likely to suffer when times are tough.

My usual Cheap Eats strategy is to have a thrifty breakfast and lunch, and then a nicer meal at suppertime. But if times are really bad, you could be looking at Cheap Eats three meals a day for a little while.

25 Cheap Eats

I consider breakfast to be interchangeable with other meals, so I've compiled a single list of our family's Cheap Eats.

1. Peanut butter and saltines
2. Oatmeal
3. Peanut butter and jelly sandwich
4. Bean burrito
5. Freezer waffles
6. Pasta and canned marinara
7. Canned soup and toast or crackers
8. Canned pasta (Only if found on sale)
9. Egg-fried rice
10. Noodle bowls (ramen, etc.)
11. Apple with peanut butter
12. Eggs and toast
13. Tuna sandwich
14. Baked potato with butter
15. Potato soup
16. Rice, frozen veggies, soy sauce
17. Beans and rice (made with canned beans)
18. Split pea soup
19. Tortilla crust pizzas
20. Pancakes
21. Pasta salad with tuna and mayo
22. Baked beans and weenies

23. Chicken and dumplings
24. Biscuits and gravy
25. Breakfast burritos with eggs and whatever you have on hand

10 ways to make mac and cheese magic

Those ubiquitous boxes of macaroni and cheese powder never fail to remind me of one of the most broke points in my life when the 33 cent (at the time) boxes were all we had standing between us and real hunger.

Now, boxed mac & cheese isn't the healthiest food in the world, but there are quite a few ways you can jazz it up, use it to extend leftovers that aren't enough to feed the whole family, or feed a large group of kids.

Go organic

If you're concerned about the icky ingredients in the cheap store brand, watch for sales on the organic brands like Annie's and Horizon. I've gotten them recently for as low as a dollar per box. If your family avoids wheat, there are also gluten-free options.

Serve it as a side dish

My kids, to this day, love a side dish of boxed mac & cheese. Personally, I prefer the homemade baked kind with a crunchy topping, but if they're willing to go cheap-o, sometimes it's nice to have that choice.

Hack homemade mac & cheese.

Speaking of the homemade kind, that stuff is pricey with all the real cheddar, cream, and butter you need. But, you can hack it inexpensively using a boxed kit as the base. Prepare the macaroni and cheese according to the instructions on the box. Butter a baking dish and spread the prepared mac & cheese into it. Stir in half a cup of cream cheese. Top it with a good quality shredded sharp cheddar and some bread crumbs, crushed potato chips, or cracker crumbs. Bake it at 350, uncovered for 25 minutes. You'll love the gooey goodness that tastes really close to homemade at a fraction of the price.

Use condiments

My kids grew up in Canada, where everyone puts ketchup on their mac & cheese. Don't knock it 'til you've tried it! I like to jazz mine up with barbecue sauce or hot sauce.

Turn it into a more flavorful side dish

Have you ever used those "Sidekick" packages of pasta? My daughter recently recreated one of her childhood favorites using white cheddar mac & cheese, garlic powder, onion powder, and parsley flakes.

Turn it into primavera

Throw in a bag of the frozen mixed vegetables of your choice while the pasta is cooking. My family likes the California mix with broccoli, cauliflower, and carrots. I like to add lots of black pepper.

Stir in a fancy cheese

Use just a little bit of a more expensive cheese to add a whole new flavor. We've tried this with smoked gouda, extra sharp cheddar, sundried tomato Havarti, fresh Parmesan, and garlic goat cheese. Remember, a little goes a long way!

Make it Mexican

Do you have leftover taco meat or leftover chili but not enough to feed the whole fam? Stir it into prepared mac & cheese and heat it all together into it's hot and bubbly. This is sort of reminiscent of Hamburger Helper, but cheaper.

Make your mac & cheese blush

Add some marinara sauce to prepared mac & cheese for a nice blush sauce. If you have leftover spaghetti sauce with meat, it's like an Italian version of Hamburger Helper.

Hide some veggies

If you're trying to hide vegetables to get your kids to eat them without complaint, cook and puree carrots or cauliflower and mix them into the sauce. They're hardly noticeable.

Sassy sauces to elevate your Cheap Eats

Just because your budget is tight and you're relegated to cheap eats, that doesn't mean you have to eat boring, bland food. A simple sauce can really jazz up the plainest of food and elevate your cheap eats to a frugally fabulous level. Whether you dip your food or pour the sauce over it, you'll get a yummy burst of flavor.

You can use whatever basic ingredients you have on hand or wish to purchase. You can go with cheap, generic ingredients or higher-quality, cleaner ingredients, depending on your budget.

Here are some of my favorite sauces.

DIY Campfire Sauce

This is a knock-off of Red Robin's Campfire Sauce. It's flippin' awesome for dipping fries, chicken nugs, or tater tots. One of my daughters also loves it on her burgers. It's also pretty tasty for dipping roasted veggies.

Ingredients

- 1/2 cup mayo

- 1/2 cup barbecue sauce (I use Sweet Baby Ray's)

Directions

1. Plop the two sauces into a bowl and mix 'em with a fork.
2. That's it.

Yum Yum Sauce

This sauce is the pinkish-white sauce you get on hibachi food, teriyaki bowls, and sushi. This is a cheap knock-off but super tasty.

Ingredients

- 1 cup of mayo
- 2 tbsp of ketchup
- 1 tbsp of white sugar
- ½ tbsp of sweet paprika
- 2 tsp of rice vinegar or cider vinegar
- 2 tsp of garlic powder

Directions

1. Plop it all in a bowl.
2. Stir it up.

If you need to make it thinner for drizzling, just add a wee bit of water, a tablespoon at a time.

Honey Mustard Sauce

This comes from my sweet mother-in-law back in Canada. She always whipped this up regularly. If you want a little bite to it, add some cayenne pepper.

Ingredients

- 2 tbsp of dry mustard
- 3 tbsp of honey
- optional: cayenne pepper

Directions

1. I'm embarrassed to call this "directions."
2. Put everything in a bowl.
3. Stir it up with a fork.

Teriyaki Sauce

I was recently in the Asian aisle of my local grocery store, and I was shocked at how much more expensive teriyaki sauce was than soy sauce. It's super cheap and easy (don't judge) to make.

Ingredients

- 1 cup of water + 1/4 cup of water
- ¼ cup of soy sauce
- 3 tbsp of brown sugar
- 1 tbsp of honey
- ½ tsp of ginger powder
- ¼ tsp garlic powder
- 2 tbsp cornstarch

Directions

1. In a cup, mix the cornstarch and the 1/4 cup of water with a fork until it's well combined. Put it aside.
2. In a saucepan, mix everything else and bring it to a simmer on low heat.
3. Stir in the cornstarch mixture and keep simmering until the teriyaki sauce reaches the desired

thickness.

Use this as a condiment on meat or veggies, or mix it up with some noodles for a tasty stirfry. It also makes a tasty dipping sauce.

Boom Boom Sauce

I first had this yummy sauce at a local breakfast place that specializes in fried chicken. (I'm from the South. Yes, fried chicken is a breakfast food.) It's a tasty dipping sauce for chicken, french fries, or other crunchy things. This sauce has a little bit of heat, but you can control how much with the amount of sriracha you put in.

Ingredients

- 1/2 cup of mayo
- 2 tbsp of ketchup
- 1 tbsp of sweet chili sauce (substitute honey if you don't have any – it's not exactly the same but it works)
- 1 tsp of garlic powder
- ¾-1 tsp of Sriracha (this is non-negotiable for Boom Boom sauce)

Directions

1. Plop everything into a bowl and mix it up with a fork.
2. That's it.

I always said that if I offered my kids dipping sauce, I could get them to eat just about anything. Sauces are a great way to dress up food that may not be the fanciest and elevate the flavor and presentation.

Fried Gnocchi

This one is from my lovely youngest daughter.

It takes some work, but it's worth every second. It takes about 3 hours to make at most, but it's worth it and freezes well. The equation I use for gnocchi is about one slightly overflowing cup of flour to one medium-sized potato.

- **Step 1:** You have to peel your potatoes and cut out any chunks you wouldn't normally shove down your gullet. Annoying and tedious, I know. It just makes it work better. I like to chop them into tiny pieces after peeling so they cook quicker. Boil the bad boys until they are fork-tender.
- **Step 2:** Once your 'taters are soft, you can put them

through a ricer, but I don't know a single person who owns one of those. So I just squish them, with the potato masher that has been in my family since way before I was born, with a few chunks of butter (around 2 tbsp).

- **Step 3:** After they're all mashed up, you'll take your flour (again, about 1 heaping cup, for one medium potato) and dump it straight onto a clean, dry counter. Make a well in the middle and add your mashed potato. Make another well and add either melted butter or a flour-water slurry. (2 tbsp. of butter, or 3 tbsp. of flour and water thoroughly mixed.) Then you're going to knead it all together until it's no longer sticky.

- **Step 4:** After you've mixed your ingredients well, you're going to want to cut the lump of dough into about 6 pieces. Once they're chopped up, you'll need to add some flour to your hands so the dough doesn't stick. Take those freshly floured hands and make a long roll of dough that's about as thick as the average thumb.

- **Step 5:** You then will bring a pot of salted water to a boil. While that's heating up, take a fork and chop the roll into about 1-inch pieces, then roll them down the fork to make a cute indent on the gnocchi. I find it turns out less gummy if I let the gnocchi sit for about 20 minutes before boiling, so I will collect all my pieces, and leave them in the order of assembly. I throw together all the gnocchi logs and proceed to dump them into the boiling water. Once they float to the top, you know they're ready.

Finished! You can leave it at that, and strain them, and add your sauce, or you can make an onion butter basil sauce to fry them. That one's always a winner, and no one would believe you if you said you made it because you had nothing else to make. It's crunchy and savory, and so good you'll have dreams about it.

Nifty thrifty things to do with tortillas

Whether you make your own from scratch or buy them at the store, regular flour tortillas are one of the thriftiest foods around.

They can be used in a wide variety of ways that go way beyond the taco, as delicious as that may be. Here's some of the fabulous fare you can create with the humble tortilla.

Burritos

You can fill a burrito with just about anything. When I lived in Mexico, there were "burrito ladies." They were little old ladies who sat on the roadside frequented by tourists and locals alike, in a lawn chair with a cooler beside them. Within that cooler was *gold*, my frugal friends. The ladies had anywhere between half a dozen to a dozen types of burritos in combos many don't think of, and I use some of these as jumping-off points for my own burritos.

My absolute favorite was the picadillo burrito. Picadillo is a Mexican stew made with ground beef, potatoes, peppers, onions, and spices all simmered together in tomato sauce. A lot of the burrito ladies also added canned corn and green beans to it. When it's simmered down to the point it's saucy instead of soupy, ladle it into your tortilla, fold, and voila!

That brings me to the fabulously frugal part about Mexican burritos: you can add a lot of inexpensive ingredients to create something delicious. Beans, rice, potatoes, drained canned veggies – as long as you season it well, your burrito will be delicious. Another thing about Mexican burritos – they rarely add cheese unless you specifically ask for it. When making your own thriftrrito, you might consider leaving out the cheese, too.

Tacos

I also became an amateur taco connoisseur when in Mexico. Like the burritos, most of the time they didn't contain cheese either.

The perfect Mexican taco is a serving of protein (whatever you happen to have on hand, well-seasoned with some chili powder and cumin works!), and some toppings. The toppings were usually diced onion, finely chopped cilantro, and a squeeze of lime. To make this the Frugalite way, you can get cilantro in a squeezy tube in your refrigerated herb section at the grocery store and you can grab lime juice in the big lime green bottle. A little of that cilantro goes a loooong way. Dice up your onion, add a teeny bit of cilantro, drizzle in some lime juice, and stir – you've got your taco-topping.

Finish it off with your favorite hot sauce, pico de Gallo, or salsa, and you've got a delicious treat.

Classic quesadillas

I've always likened quesadillas to Mexican grilled cheese sandwiches. You can make them super simple – just cheese and tortillas cooked on your stovetop, or you can go all in, adding veggies and meat to your quesadilla.

I've found the trick to getting melty goodness is to put a lid on your skillet and leave it open-faced initially. Then, once your cheese is melted, either fold the tortilla over or top it with a second one. Then squash it down with your spatula, flip, and put the lid back on.

Breakfast quesadillas

This is basically the same as classic quesadillas, but you fill it with delicious breakfast things. I like to use scrambled eggs, veggies, and sausage or bacon as my filling along with the cheese. Dip it in sour cream or salsa.

Wraps

You can wrap just about anything! If you're Southern, you'll probably put ranch dressing on it. I like to use a combo of meat, lettuce, tomato, and any other yummy ingredient I have kicking around.

Bunuelos

Oh my gosh. This is a fast-fried tortilla smothered in cinnamon sugar. You simply throw some butter or cooking oil in your skillet and get it hot. Then drop your tortilla in. It'll start to puff up, and that's when you know it's time to flip it. It takes about 30 seconds to 2 minutes per side, depending on your skillet and how high you have the heat. When it's golden brown on each side, move the tortilla to a plate lined with a paper towel and bury that bad boy in your cinnamon sugar mix. Meanwhile, start working on your next tortilla.

Shake the excess topping off your first tortilla and move it to another plate. Repeat with the rest of your tortillas. You may think you'll just eat one. It's more like one-half-dozen, they're that good.

Soup or salad topping

Mmmm.... you can either bake or fry strips of tortilla, then crumble them onto your soup or salad for some southwestern crunch.

Personal pizza

I have used tortillas as the base of personal pizzas for years. This was an awesome way to get my kids pizza without spending a fortune on takeout.

Breakfast burritos

This is a lot like the breakfast quesadilla, except you're simply wrapping your breakfast food in a flour tortilla to make a portable pocket of breakfast for your commute.

Cups

You can make yummy tortilla cups that look fancy enough to dazzle guests on a dime. Always cook your tortilla cups before filling them, or the results won't be great.

Preheat your oven to 350. Then spray a muffin tin with cooking spray. Place a tortilla into the muffin cup and fold it in to form a little bowl. Bake it for about 10-12 minutes or until the whole thing is crisp.

Take the cups out carefully to cool on a baking rack. Then fill 'em to your heart's content. I like to make mini taco salads in these.

Pinwheels

Pinwheels are just tightly-wound wraps cut into slices. The trick is to use something sort of thick to keep the slices together. Seasoned cream cheese works beautifully for this.

Mexican Pizza

My kids loved, loved, LOVED this. You can use a cast iron skillet for it or a round cake pan.

Grease your vessel and lay down a flour tortilla. Top it with a layer of refried beans, salsa, and cheese. Plop down another tortilla and repeat. I like to make 3-4 layers of this. Cover it with foil and bake it at 375F for 20 minutes. Then take the foil off, sprinkle it with cheese, and bake it for five more minutes.

Let it cool for 10 minutes, then slice it like a pie. You can also add in ground beef if you want a meaty recipe.

Tortillas ideas (it sort of rhymes...right?)

When I asked my daughter how she used tortillas, she compiled the following comprehensive list:

- Peanut butter and jelly roll up
- Banana peanut butter roll-up (a quick, easy breakfast for the kiddos.)

- Peanut butter and honey roll up
- Peanut butter and Nutella roll up
- Peanut butter pizza (This is a term my friend's son coined years ago. Basically, you just slather peanut butter and sometimes jam and eat it open-faced, pizza style!)
- Pan-fried s'mores (a handful of marshmallows, a dab of Nutella or some chocolate chips, and if you want to get *really* fancy, a little peanut butter to spice it up. Cook it all just like you would a normal quesadilla
- Tortilla omelet
- Tortilla-baked eggs (grease a pan, lay down tortillas, and crack an egg on top of each – bake for 5 minutes at 375F)
- Stacked tortilla casserole
- "Pizza pockets" – Kinda like a quesadilla, but with pizza toppings for fillings
- Enchiladas
- Tortilla soup
- Taquitos (tightly rolled mini-tacos that are fried or baked til crisp)
- Tostadas (it's like an open-faced taco)
- Homemade chips in the oven
- Caramel apple taquitos
- Tortilla cinnamon buns (spread them with butter and cinnamon sugar filling, then wrap them up like pinwheels – can be baked or not)
- A quick, easy replacement for tart shells in a pinch

And finally...the ultimate money-saving tortilla hack, chilaquiles

Do you have a bag of tortilla chips that got stale because someone didn't close them up after grabbing a handful? Or some soft tortillas that dried out and can no longer be used for burritos or soft tacos? Then you should consider using them up the way they do in Mexico with a dish called chilaquiles. (Chill-ah-KEY-lays)

I love making meals out of stuff that lots of folks would just throw away and chilaquiles is just such a dish. I had them at a restaurant my first breakfast in Mexico and was immediately hooked. The plate I had was served with beans, potatoes, shredded meat, plus some guacamole for good measure.

They can be served in several different ways but first, let's talk about what they are. They're traditionally served as a breakfast food, and you can order either chilaquiles rojas (red) or chilaquiles verde (green). It all depends on the sauce you want. It sort of reminds me of a cross between nachos and enchiladas.

Apologies in advance to my Mexican friends for any mistakes I may have made interpreting this recipe. All errors are mine and mine alone.

How to Make Chilaquiles

Here's how to make chilaquiles.

Ingredients

- Tortillas or tortilla chips
- Enchilada Sauce – you can use either red or green and don't be afraid to use canned sauce!

Toppings of your choice:

- Cheese (either traditional Mexican cheese or shredded cheddar or Monterey Jack)
- Crema or sour cream
- Fresh or freeze-dried cilantro
- Chopped onions
- Diced tomatoes
- Salsa or pico de gallo
- Guacamole

NOTE: I often leave off the cheese and crema or only use a teeny bit because dairy and I are not really friends. It's still delicious.

Directions:

- If you are using soft tortillas, you'll need to bake or fry them until they're a bit crisp.
- Then, make (or heat up) the enchilada sauce of your choice in a large saucepan or skillet.
- Stir in your tortilla chips until they're coated with sauce.
- Dish them onto a plate, sprinkle them with crumbled cheese and crema (or sour cream), and any other toppings of your choice, and BOOM – that's it – you've made chilaquiles.

To make the meal more substantial, you can serve it with eggs, beans, or meat. Some restaurants serve it with a sunnyside-up egg right on top. And don't tie yourself down only to breakfast. You can throw some ground beef or chorizo on top and serve it with pico de gallo for a nacho-esque dinnertime meal.

Fun fact: some Mexican diners serve a batch of red-sauced chilaquiles and a batch of green sauced ones and call them Divorce Chilaquiles!

Stretch your food

Another way to make your Eats good and Cheap is to stretch them with less expensive ingredients. Here are a few ideas for stretching a smaller amount of an expensive food with a less expensive food.

- Serve leftover meat in gravy that you put over mashed potatoes.
- Add extra rice, noodles, barley, or potatoes to your soup or casserole.
- Mix cooked beans into ground beef to make it go further while bumping up the fiber.
- Serve hearty homemade bread or biscuits as a side dish with meals.
- Add shredded cabbage to your salads to make the more expensive ingredients go further.
- Serve food from the stove. Dish out the plates yourself and take the plates to the table. You can put inexpensive side dishes like pilaf or potatoes on the table. This slows down people going back repeatedly for the more expensive dish because they're less likely to go into the kitchen to get it unless they're actually hungry. If it's within reach, they'll just keep eating it.
- Use meat as a condiment instead of a main dish when times are tight.

Focus the bulk of your meals on less expensive ingredients and make the more expensive parts the highlight.

How to get your family on board with Cheap Eats

When you change your eating style dramatically, you generally need to have a conversation with your family members. I find you get fewer complaints when you discuss things as opposed to laying down the law. Make it a bargain. "If we eat X for breakfast every day this week, then we can afford to do pizza day at school."

Cheap Eats can be a real budget saver when it comes to food or when you're trying to get through a tight spot. Think about what YOU can concoct for a buck a serving and create your own Cheap Eats.

Pantry Raid

Let's discuss that shelf-stable food you may have been avoiding.

I'm talking about things like tuna fish, canned fruits and vegetables, tomatoes, jam/jelly, and peanut butter. The stuff that most folks don't want to eat til they're right down to the wire. Once you read this, you may ask yourself what in the daylights you've been waiting for. You may say, "It's canned goods for me, now and forevahhhhh!" (Okay, you probably won't say that, but at least the idea of them won't trigger your gag reflex.)

Peanut Butter

Here are some tasty-and-cheap things to do with PB that my oldest daughter compiled. If you like crunchy, you're wrong, but I still love you. You can use any nut butter for these, and if you're allergic to nuts, sun butter (made from sunflower seeds) is a good substitution.)

1. Apple slices dipped in peanut butter

2. PB and jam roll-ups
3. PB and banana roll-ups
4. PB and honey roll-ups
5. PB and brown sugar roll-ups
6. Simple peanut butter stir-fry (this was actually my favorite way to eat Chinese food as a kid. When it's time to add your sauce to your stir fry, try using 2 tbsp. soya sauce, 2 tbsp. peanut butter, a pinch of ginger and garlic, and a little something sweet, such as 1 tbsp. of brown sugar.)
7. Peanut butter-banana smoothie
8. PB strawberry smoothie (this one tastes like a peanut butter and jelly sandwich)
9. PB and honey sandwich
10. PB and jam sandwich
11. PB and banana sandwich
12. PB and crackers
13. PB by the spoon full
14. A spoon of PB with a few chocolate chips
15. PB cookies
16. Vegan peanut butter-banana ice cream (blend one frozen banana and 1 tbsp. of peanut butter, and you've got a bowl ready to go!)
17. PB s'mores
18. PB frosting (just switch half or all of the butter you use in your frosting recipe for peanut butter)
19. Add a scoop of PB to your oatmeal
20. PB burgers (I kid you not, it's actually a thing, they're

called 'sticky burgers,' and they're delicious)

21. PB and celery (pop some raisins on top, and you'll have ants on a log)
22. Chocolate PB pie
23. A drizzle on ice cream
24. PB on pancakes, crepes, or waffles
25. PB chicken satay (see the recipe for peanut sauce in Chapter 4)
26. PB smoothie bowl
27. PB and bacon sandwich (it's better than it sounds)
28. PB on toast (or a bagel, or an English muffin)
29. Grilled PB (basically the same as grilled cheese, just with peanut butter inside)
30. PB on a slice of banana bread
31. PB on a brownie
32. PB on a cookie
33. PB on an Oreo (this is one of my favorites)
34. PB and graham crackers
35. PB and marshmallow sandwich
36. Dessert pizza with PB as the sauce and chocolate chips as the topping
37. Drizzle PB over popcorn
38. Homemade PB cups
39. Mix PB and yogurt for a tasty fruit dip.
40. Put a little PB at the bottom of your ice cream cone to prevent any ice cream from leaking out.

Tuna

My peanut-butter-loving daughter has also become a fan of tuna, and she put together these ideas. If you don't like tuna or you happen to have canned ham flakes kicking around, it can be used in exactly the same way as tuna – just sub it in.

Tuna. For most people, you either love it or you hate it. As a kid, I was in the latter group. Over the last year or so, I've started to like it pretty well. I wouldn't go as far as to say I love it, but I definitely like it now.

In the U.S., the average cost of a good quality can of tuna is $1.50 or $2, give or take a little. Whatever country you may be in, there are a few things you want to look for. These things will make sure you're getting a healthier and better quality cut of the fish. You either want to look for "chunk" or "solid." You can find flakes of tuna and other types, but when you go with a chunk or solid, you're assuring that your getting tuna from the same fish, and the same area of the fish. Anything else, and you could just be getting the leftover scraps, which isn't nearly as good for you. (Think a hot dog compared to a steak).

The other thing you're going to want to keep an eye on is that you're getting tuna canned in water. When you get it canned in oil, it brings down the healthiness, it, at least in my opinion, isn't nearly as tasty, and it's getting loaded with salt and more unhealthy saturated fats.

How often should we eat tuna?

Sometimes, this is something people think of, sometimes, it doesn't even cross a person's mind. The FDA has some guidelines on how often children and women should eat fish in general. This is because some fish is very high in mercury, which can build up in your body over time. High levels of mercury can harm heart health and brain function. To sum it up though, for kids 7 and under, it's not recommended to have more than one can a week. For adults, it's recommended that you max it out at 2-3 servings (cans) a week.

What's so great about tuna?

For every ounce (28 grams) of tuna packed in water and strained, you're going to find 1 gram of fat, 6 grams of protein, and a mere 24 calories. That might not sound like a ton of protein, but when you think about the fact that the average can of tuna in the states is 5 ounces, (6 ounces in Canada), you've got at least 30 grams of protein for less than 150 calories.

And if 30 grams of protein doesn't seem like a lot, put it in perspective: a Big Mac at Mcdonald's has over 500 calories, yet only 25 grams of protein. Not to mention, tuna has way fewer preservatives, chemicals, sodium, and other unhealthy things.

Now, let's get into some recipes!

Tuna Salad

This is probably one of the most basic things you can do with tuna. It's super easy, cheap, and completely customizable. All you really need are a few thrifty ingredients;

1. Tuna
2. Mayonnaise
3. Salt & Pepper to taste

What'd I tell you? Easy right? The ratio I find I like the most is one tablespoon of mayo to 2 ounces of tuna. But, it's completely customizable to your personal preferences! Now, this is just the basics. Let's see how we can spice it up a little and give it a flavor punch. (Please note; I still add the mayo salt and pepper, I just use these to heighten the flavor.)

Fresh and Dilly – To me, there is just something about dill, be it dried or fresh, that just brings a light freshness to any meal. I personally love to add a teaspoon of dill, and a teaspoon of lemon juice to my tuna, as well as a small sprig of green onion from my garden. I just find it takes the canned and bland food and really livens it up.

Embrace the Heat – Another fun one is adding a little hot sauce into the mix. My go-to is usually Frank's Red Hot Sauce. It's cheap, and it just brings that nice cayenne pepper taste to the front. Mixed with the mayo, it's a perfect pairing!

In a Pickle – Or, maybe more accurately, the pickle is in the tuna. I like to take a little bit of dill pickle, dice it up finely, (I usually do about 2 tablespoons), and add it in. That, mixed with the mayo, gives it an almost tartar sauce-like quality which I absolutely love.

Tuna Melt

Okay, so we all know how to make a tuna sandwich. You take one of the above tuna salad recipes and slap it on a couple of slices of bread and there you go. An easy, typical, (and slightly boring) lunch. But, what if, with just a little effort, you could turn it into something fancy? Tuna melts are the best way to do it!

It's super easy. First, take your bread (buns work great as well), and you're going to want to toast it. I recommend in the oven at 425F for about 10 minutes. Slather a little butter or margarine on beforehand for a perfect golden toast. While that's in the oven, take your preferred tuna salad recipe and mix it up. Also, shred a little cheese too – I prefer cheddar, marble, or mozzarella.

Once the bread is done toasting, pull it out of the oven, spread the tuna evenly on each piece, and top with that shredded (or sliced) cheese. Put it back in the oven for another 10 minutes, or until the cheese gets all melty, and bam! you've got yourself a delicious-looking gourmet tuna melt!

Tuna Casserole

Don't forget our ultimate frugal casserole formula. Tuna makes a great protein to add to this! One of my go-tos is to make tuna casserole with rice, but it's also great used with other grains like pasta or quinoa. (I haven't tried it with potatoes myself, but who knows, that might be tasty too!)

My standard recipe is:

- 6 cups cooked rice or cooked pasta (if pasta, I typically go for something like macaroni noodles)

- 2 cans of tuna (I prefer the tuna that is stored in water)
- 2 cans of cream of mushroom soup** (10.5oz/ 284mL)

I know not everyone likes mushrooms, so if you want to swap the soup, both cream of broccoli and cream of celery work just as well.

For vegetables, I like to add peas, corn, or carrots. Mix it all together and bake until hot. And, if you're like me and love cheese, this is a great dish to sprinkle a little on top of and melt in the oven until bubbly.

And that's it, a meal for many with minimal effort!

A few more ideas

Here are just a few short other ideas if you're still wanting more.

- **Pasta Salad with Tuna** – this is super easy to make. Just add a can of strained tuna into your standard pasta salad recipe, and you've got an extra source of a little protein.
- **Tuna Wraps/Sandwiches** – these ones are pretty self-explanatory and probably a go-to for many tuna eaters, but, though I should still write them down.

And, if you're looking for something new, try it with one of the tuna salad recipes listed above.

- **Lettuce Salad** – Add a can to your lettuce salad. It's a great alternative to chicken, and just as filling. I love it with a bit of ranch dressing.
- **Try a Lettuce Wrap** – Instead of tortilla or bread, try switching it up and adding a little extra veggies, and put it in a piece of lettuce instead.
- **Tuna and Crackers** – Try your favorite tuna salad recipe and just add it to crackers. This makes for a great quick-and-easy lunch.
- **Tuna Cakes** – I don't have a go-to recipe for tuna cakes, but there are tons. And by cake, I mean tuna, mixed with flour (and I think eggs) and pan-fried in oil until hot and crispy.

So many options

With tuna, there are so many options. There are almost endless recipes you can try. There are also so many health benefits. If you haven't tried adding tuna to your weekly meal plan yet, I recommend starting the next time you go to the store. There really isn't a reason not to!

Tasty Ways to Eat Canned Vegetables – Really!

If you're anything like me, your heart does not go pitter-patter at the idea of opening a can of veggies and saying, "Buon appetite!" Also, if you're anything like me, you have a hefty stash of them that you bought on sale. So, how can you use them (and get your family to come back for seconds?)

Here are a few concoctions I make with canned veggies that my family and I enjoy. Consider working them into your repertoire to use up those cans collecting dust in your pantry. Here are some things I make, which include canned veggies, that my whole family enjoys. Please note that these aren't all the healthiest dishes in the world, but they're hearty, inexpensive, filling, and tasty if that's what you're looking for in a recipe.

Christmas Beans

I made this one long ago Christmas as an alternative to green bean casserole, and now we eat it regularly (but we still call them Christmas Beans).

Ingredients:

- 2 cans of green beans (NOT french cut – the regular ones) well-drained
- 3 strips of bacon
- 2/3 cup of brown sugar
- 1 tablespoon of apple cider vinegar
- 1 tablespoon of minced garlic
- 1 tablespoon of minced onion
- Optional: 1 tsp of flour or cornstarch to thicken your sauce
- Salt and pepper as needed

Directions:

1. Fry up your bacon in a big skillet – I like mine pretty well done but I leave it soft in this initial step.
2. Next, remove the bacon to a plate. Once it cools, chop it up into tasty bite-sized pieces.
3. Whisk in your sugar, vinegar, garlic, and onion and let it get bubbly. If it needs thickening, whisk in your flour now.
4. When it's the consistency you like, stir in your drained green beans and your bacon. Let it get carmelized and wonderful and heated through – about 3 minutes.
5. Remove it from the heat and season it as desired.

Beef and Vegetable Soup

You can use any kind of ground meat for this soup.

Ingredients:

- 1 large can of V-8 or V-8 type juice
- 1 pound of ground meat
- 1/2 an onion, diced
- 3 cloves of garlic, minced
- 1 can of green beans, including liquid
- 1 can of corn, including liquid
- 1 can of peas and carrots, including liquid
- Optional: add a can of potatoes and a can of tomatoes, peppers, and onions (like Ro-Tel for my Southern friends) – you can also add some pasta during the last 10 minutes of cooking time
- 2 tablespoons of an Italian spice blend

Directions:

1. In a large stockpot, brown your ground meat, along with the onion and garlic, until it's cooked through.
2. Turn down the heat and add in all the rest of your ingredients. Let it simmer on the stovetop or dump the entire thing into your crockpot. The longer it

cooks, the tastier it is.

Picadillo

You can use picadillo as a hearty stew, or as an enchilada or burrito filling. Please remember I'm terrible at measuring and tend to cook by "feel" more than by recipe. But the instructions below should give you enough to go on. Feel free to tweak this recipe to fit your own likes and dislikes.

When I lived in Mexico, I was kind of surprised that the only canned veggies I could easily find were mixed vegetables and corn. Once I tried picadillo, I completely understood why they liked canned mixed veggies so much. A friend there brought me some picadillo stew when I had Covid, and I unlocked the world of picadillo. Leftover stew or a version with just a bit of tomato sauce instead of a giant can of tomatoes and broth is used to stuff burritos, enchiladas, and just as a one-dish meal.

Maria never gave me a specific recipe, but this is how she showed me to make it. It seems like a ton of work, but it's really not bad at all.

Ingredients:

- 1-2 pounds of ground beef
- 2 cans of mixed veggies (the kind with potatoes)
- 1 can of black beans
- Finely minced garlic
- 1/2 an onion, minced
- Cumin, chili powder, salt, seasoning salt, and oregano to taste
- 1 small can of tomato sauce

Directions:

1. In a large skillet, fry up your ground beef, garlic, and onion until the meat is cooked through. I prefer to get it a little bit brown because I like the texture better. When it's almost done, season it with cumin, chili powder, and salt.
2. While the meat is cooking, drain two cans of mixed veggies. I usually sit a sieve in a bowl for this.
3. Remove the cooked meat mixture from your skillet and immediately put in your mixed veggies. Stir them up in the beef drippings. (I never said this was healthy, right?)
4. Fry the veggies for about 10 minutes until they're nicely browned. Season them with salt and oregano.
5. When the veggies are done, stir in your meat

mixture and your tomato sauce. Remove it from the heat and let it sit for a few minutes before serving.

Use this mixture to stuff your enchiladas or your burritos. If you are making it as a stew, add a large can of crushed tomatoes once everything is fried up and let it simmer for a while.

Shepherd's Pie

This is something I learned to make when I lived in Canada. Of course, it's officially only shepherd's pie if your meat is ground lamb – I believe it's called cottage pie with other meats. We just used the name "shepherd's pie" in a universal sense.

Ingredients:

- 1 lb of ground meat
- 1/2 an onion, diced
- 2 cloves of garlic, minced
- 1 can of peas, drained
- 1 can of carrots, , drained
- 1 can of corn, drained
- 1/2 a packet of brown gravy mix
- 4 cups of mashed potatoes, prepared

- 2 tbsp of butter (optional)
- salt and pepper to taste

Directions:

- In an ovenproof skillet, brown your meat, onion, and garlic. (I use my trusty cast-iron frying pan.)
- Stir in your gravy mix to coat the meat, then add your canned veggies (make sure they're drained!)
- Spread your mashed potatoes over the top of this concoction. Add a dollop of butter and a sprinkle of black pepper on top.
- Bake it at 375F for 45 minutes. I usually cover it with foil the first half hour then remove the foil for the last bit.

Some people like to add cheese to the mashed potatoes but we rarely do. My whole family likes this with a drizzle of ketchup at the table.

Corn Casserole

Super easy and mostly from pantry ingredients! Nearly all of these recipes call for an egg but because one of my children is allergic, I always left it out and it still turned out great.

Ingredients:

- 1 box of Jiffy cornbread mix
- 1 can of creamed corn
- 1 can of whole-kernel corn, drained
- 1 cup of sour cream OR cream cheese
- 1/2 cup of melted butter

Directions:

1. In a bowl, mix the cornbread mix, butter, and sour cream/cream cheese together until it's incorporated.
2. Stir in the w cans of corn.
3. Pop it all in a buttered baking dish and bake it at 350 until a knife comes out clean, approximately 45 minutes.

For a different flavor, you can add cheddar cheese and a wee can of drained, diced chili peppers.

Peas and potatoes

This falls into the category of not fancy but very tasty and filling. You can season it differently to go with different meals but I've just provided the basics here.

Ingredients:

- 1 can of potatoes, drained
- 1 can of green peas, drained
- 1/2 onion, diced
- 1 teaspoon of rubbed thyme
- 2 tbsp of butter
- salt and pepper to taste

Directions:

1. Melt 1 tbsp. of butter in a large skillet and cook your onion until it's translucent.
2. Add the rest of the butter, then crank up the heat a little and add the potatoes and peas.
3. Put the lid on and set a timer for 4 minutes.
4. Stir your mixture – it should be lightly browned on the skillet side. Add your thyme, salt, and pepper, then pop the lid on for 2 more minutes.

Serve as is, or top it with extra butter and a spoonful of sour cream.

5 insanely delicious thrifty things to make with canned crushed tomatoes

One of the most versatile canned goods in your frugal scratch-cooking pantry is crushed tomatoes.

I'm never without dozens of cans of them. Every time they go on sale I stock up. They are the thrifty basis of many delicious and hearty meals. I'll share a few of my favorites with you, including my up-to-now closely-guarded salsa recipe. (Shhh – don't tell anyone!)

Marinara Sauce

- 1 28-ounce can of crushed tomatoes
- 1 tbsp of olive oil
- 1 large carrot
- 1/2 large onion
- 6 cloves of garlic
- 1/3 large bell pepper

Add seasoning to taste:

- sea salt
- oregano
- basil

- smoked paprika

Also add the teeniest, tiniest pinch of clove – trust me.

1. Use your food processor to mince the carrot, onion, garlic, and pepper.
2. Heat the olive oil in a non-reactive stock pot then add your minced veggies. Saute them until they're golden and fragrant.
3. Add your crushed tomatoes, then stir in your seasonings.
4. Simmer it for a couple of hours to meld the flavors well.

Serve this alone over pasta or add ground meat, meatballs, and extra veggies. You can also use this marinara in baked pasta dishes like lasagna.

7 can soup

I love a hearty vegetable soup and this recipe is made totally from canned goods and seasonings.

- 1 can of crushed tomatoes
- 1 can of white kidney beans, including liquid
- 1 can of green beans, including liquid
- 1 can of peas and carrots, including liquid

- 1 can of potatoes, including liquid
- 1 can of corn, including liquid
- 1 can of RoTel (tomatoes, peppers, and onions)

Seasonings:

I like to use my homemade Italian spice blend or my Mexican spice blend depending on my mood.

Directions:

Okay, I feel kind of bad about even really calling this "directions."

- Dump all the cans in together, add your seasonings, and simmer it for an hour or so to let the flavors blend.

Serve it with some fresh, crusty bread or crackers.

V-6

Break out your blender for this one. If you're a fan of those canned vegetable juices like V-8 here's how you can make your own. I often make this with excess garden produce.

- 1 can of crushed tomatoes
- 1 bell pepper
- 1 small onion
- 2 cloves of garlic
- 1 carrot
- 1 stalk of celery
- a dash of salt
- a dash of lemon juice

Pop everything into your blender or food processor and whiz that stuff up until it's a thick liquid. I think it tastes much better cold. You can also use this as an uber-nutritious soup base.

Tomato Basil Soup

This is so far away from those red and white cans of tomato basil soup that it might as well be from another galaxy.

Ingredients

- 1 can of crushed tomatoes
- 2 tbsp of butter
- 1/2 onion, diced
- 2 cloves of garlic, minced

- salt and pepper to taste
- a metric crapton of basil, fresh or dried (not to be confused with an imperial crapton)
- optional: sour cream and vegetable broth

Directions

1. In a non-reactive stockpot, saute your garlic and onion in the butter.
2. Stir in your crushed tomatoes. If you find this soup too thick for your liking, you can thin it down with vegetable broth.
3. Bring the soup to a simmer, then add most of your basil, as well as your salt and pepper.
4. Let it simmer for 20-30 minutes, covered, stirring frequently.
5. If you choose to add sour cream, stir in a dollop now. Garnish the soup with your remaining basil.

Your delicious soup is only awaiting the arrival of your hot grilled cheese sandwich on the plate beside it.

Salsa

Even before I spent a year in Mexico, I had a roommate from that southerly nation during my misspent youth. He planted a little garden specific to salsa and taught all of us living in the big house how to make it. I've tweaked the recipe over the years to be able to use canned tomatoes during the winter.

This does require some fresh ingredients for best results, but the tasty concoction is still less expensive than a jar of not-very-authentic stuff that rhymes with "mostitos."

Ingredients:

- 1 can of crushed tomatoes
- 1 bunch of fresh cilantro
- 1/2 bell pepper, any color
- 1/2 large onion
- 1 jalapeno (or more if you like it really spicy)
- 1 tbsp minced garlic
- 2 tbsp lemon or lime juice (alternatively, 1 tsp of lemon pepper seasoning)
- 1 tbsp chili powder
- optional: salt to taste
- optional but it is so so so good: a splash of tequila – yep, tequila

Directions:

1. Place a strainer over a bowl and dump your can of

crushed tomatoes to strain while you're prepping the rest of the veggies.

2. Pull the leaves off your cilantro bundle after washing it well. Don't include the stems in your recipe because they're bitter.

3. In batches, process your onion, jalapeno, bell pepper, and cilantro. I don't totally puree it but i get the pieces very small. This is not a chunky salsa, but a relatively smooth one.

4. In another bowl, add your somewhat strained tomatoes and your finely chopped veggies. Stir in your garlic, chili powder, and salt, if you're adding any.

5. Then add your lime juice and tequila and tell me how flippin' good this salsa is!

This is my go-to for any family event or Mexican food night. If you insist on chucks you can add one can of drained diced tomatoes and chop your veggies by hand.

Ways to eat jam that have nothing to do with bread

Do you have jars and jars of jam sitting there in your pantry, enough to make you say, "There's not enough toast in the world for all this?"

Well, I have ideas for that jam, and they have nothing to do with any bread product whatsoever. I make jam every year like it's my job. I sometimes add to this stash with a good clearance sale. Some of it gets given away at the holidays, some of it gets used for standard jam purposes, and the rest gets used in other creative ways.

Here are some interesting ways to use jam or jelly that don't require you to spread it on anything.

Spice it up. This right here is a family favorite. Heat up your jam and add in some fresh finely chopped jalapeno. Pop it back in the fridge to let it cool off, then serve it over a brick of cream cheese or some backed Brie. I've tried it with multiple flavors of jam. Our favorites have been peach, apricot, raspberry, and blackberry.

Grape jelly meatballs. Family fave, right here. In a crockpot, add half a cup of grape jelly, half a cup of your favorite barbecue sauce, a splash of soy sauce, and some garlic powder. Either make meatballs or buy frozen ones. Add the full cooked meatballs and heat it all up on low for 3-4 hours.

Add it to yogurt. Make your own "fruit-on-the-bottom".

Make thumbprint cookies. This works well with cookies that aren't overly sweet, like shortbread.

Use it to glaze carrots

Add it to smoothies

Turn it into syrup. Heat it up over low heat until it reaches a liquid texture. If you need to, add some apple or grape juice to it to make it more liquid-y. Use this on pancakes or waffles.

Top an ice cream sundae with it. You can turn it into syrup or use it as is.

Add it to oatmeal.

Make a fruity trifle. I like to do this if I find an angel food cake on the last-day-of-sale aisle. Heat up your entire jar of jam. Cut up the angel food cake into cubes. In a large glass bowl, layer cake, jam, whipped cream, cake, jam, whipped cream, until you're all out of cake, jam, and whipped cream. You can serve it immediately or put it in the fridge to let it all meld deliciously. I could eat an entire bowl of this.

Make dipping sauce for chicken strips. Heat up some raspberry jam and present it as a fancy dipping sauce.

Fill turnovers with jam and cream cheese. Go back to the pocket recipe in Chapter 6 for instructions.

Glaze a ham with it. I like this with cherry, peach, or apricot jam, although I'm sure many others would be likewise delicious.

Use it as a base for cranberry sauce. My mother-in-law used to mix extra tart cranberry sauce with strawberry jam.

Top some cheesecake with a dollop.

Add it to grilled cheese. (Okay, there's bread, but this is different!) Before making your sandwich, spread the inside of the bread with jam like fig or raspberry. Add some bold cheese and perhaps some salty ham or prosciutto. Grill away and be sure to make extra.

Add it to a charcuterie tray. You can add the spiced-up version or the regular version to your next work of meat-and-cheese art. Jam on crackers is the bomb-diggity.

Sweeten up some barbecue sauce.

See? Jam is not just for biscuits!

Cooking and baking without eggs

With the price of eggs, you might be thinking about cutting out recipes that require them for cooking and baking. I have good news: that may not be necessary.

I've navigated a world without eggs my entire life. First, my father was allergic to eggs when I was growing up, and then later, my youngest daughter was allergic to them. We became pros at dodging food that contained egg in meals out or cooked by other people, and I also learned how to bake and cook without them.

Here are my best tips for how to cook and bake without eggs.

There are two ways to cook and bake without eggs:

- Learn to use substitutes for eggs in your existing recipes.
- Look for recipes that don't contain eggs in the first place.

I've used both of these strategies.

Egg substitutes

Let me be absolutely clear that the little carton of "egg substitute" in the dairy fridge at your local store is really just eggs that you don't have to break. I find that name very misleading, and people have mistakenly thought it was safe for my daughter to eat things made with "egg substitutes," sending us straight to the ER.

And it should go without saying (but for some folks, I need to add this) these work as an ingredient, not the star of the dish. You can't make an applesauce omelet or fried baking soda.

There are quite a few egg substitutes that work well in standard recipes, though. Some of them are thrifty and some are not. Here are the ones that I have used regularly for years.

Egg wash

You can use any kind of cooking oil in place of egg wash on a baked good. I use coconut oil on sweet foods and olive or sunflower oil on savory foods.

Applesauce

Unsweetened applesauce works in both sweet and savory baked goods. I find that it makes the dish a little bit moister and airier too. Use 1/4 cup of applesauce per egg.

Baking soda

You can mix this with oil or white vinegar, depending on what kind of recipe in which you're using it. The standard is one teaspoon of soda to one tablespoon of liquid per egg. Use vinegar for things that you want to be light and fluffy, like pancakes. Use oil for things that can be a little more dense, like dinner rolls, quickbreads, or cake.

Aquafaba

This super-fancy-sounding thing is just chickpea liquid. So the next time you're draining a can of chickpeas, save the liquid to use in place of egg whites. 3 tablespoons equals one egg or two egg whites.

Flax seed

This has long been a go-to for me because it works extremely well in both sweet and savory dishes and it doesn't cost much money at all. Either buy it in powder form or whiz it up in your food processor to get a powder. For the equivalent of one egg, add one tablespoon of ground flax seed to 3 tablespoons of water and let it sit for 15-20 minutes.

Yogurt

I like to use this in dense recipes like banana bread and zucchini bread. 1/4 cup of yogurt is the equivalent of one egg. I feel like this adds a lot of richness to my recipes. I've also regularly used it in casseroles and other savory dishes that call for egg and won't be weird with a touch of dairy.

Soda water

Plain old fizzy water works really well for recipes that you want to be light and fluffy. Use a quarter cup for one egg. Depending on what you're making, you could also use soda pop. For example, if you were making orange-cranberry muffins and had some orange soda pop kicking around, it would work well and enhance the orange-y flavor. You can also add Coca-Cola or Dr. Pepper to chocolate cake mix with tasty results.

I know there are tons of other egg substitutes out there but these are tried and true for me.

Recipes that don't have eggs to start with

First things first, there are a surprising number of recipes that just don't have eggs to begin with. Start with those as opposed to diving straight into the world of substitutions.

For example, a lot of Great Depression recipes omitted the eggs (and other expensive ingredients) simply because folks couldn't afford them. So-called "Depression Cake" doesn't contain eggs, milk, or butter and it's absolutely delicious. It's easy to find recipes for this cake online.

Shortbread cookies are also egg-free from the get-go. Also, things like apple crisp (or other fruit crisps) don't have egg in the topping. It's made from just oats, sugar, and butter.

Sometimes visiting the recipes of other countries can help. For example, Russian tea cakes are egg-free, as are Mexican wedding cookies. Nahnkhatai are highly spiced cookies from India. Melomakaronos are traditional Greek Christmas honey cookies. Ma'amouls are tasty Lebanese date cookies. I'm sure there are others, but these are the ones that come to mind.

Some vegan recipes are super-thrifty, as long as they don't require wildly exotic ingredients and substitutions.

Easy, thrifty cookies from pantry ingredients

Here are some simple, no-egg cookie recipes for cookies that are right from the pantry (with the exception of butter.) The omission of eggs makes these cookies easily attainable from pantry goods.

Basic "chip" cookie recipe

We have used all sorts of goodies in this recipe – for Christmas baking this year we used white chocolate chips and dried cranberries. This recipe makes the best light, soft chocolate chip cookies I've ever had, too!

Ingredients:

- 1 cup of brown sugar
- 1/2 cup of melted coconut oil
- 1/2 cup plain nonfat yogurt
- 2 tsp vanilla extract
- 1- 3/4 cups flour
- 1/2 tsp baking soda
- 1/2 tsp salt
- 2 cups of chips (chocolate, white chocolate, Skor –

whatever!)

Directions:

1. Preheat the oven to 375 degrees F (190 degrees C).
2. Grease cookie sheets (I use coconut oil for this)
3. With a fork, mix the sugar, vanilla, coconut oil and yogurt until light and fluffy.
4. Sift together the flour, baking soda, and salt and then stir into the creamed mixture until incorporated.
5. then mix in chocolate chips. Drop by rounded teaspoonfuls 2 inches apart onto the prepared cookie sheets.
6. Bake for 8 to 10 minutes in the preheated oven, until the edges begin to brown. Cool for a minute on the cookie sheets before removing to wire racks to cool completely.

Ginger molasses cookies

Ingredients:

- 2 cups of flour
- 1/2 cup of white sugar

- 2 Tbsp. ginger powder
- 1/3 cup molasses
- 1/3 cup of applesauce
- 1/3 cup melted coconut oil (you can't taste the coconut at ALL – don't worry!)
- 1 tsp salt
- 1 tsp cinnamon
- 1/2 tsp of powdered cloves
- 1 tsp vanilla extract
- 1/2 tsp baking soda
- 2 tsp baking powder

Directions:

1. Preheat the oven to 375 degrees F/ 190 degrees C.
2. In a large mixing bowl, combine the dry ingredients with a fork: flour, sugar, ginger powder, cinnamon, salt, baking soda/powder.
3. In a second bowl, combine the melted coconut oil, applesauce, molasses, and vanilla extract.
4. Stir the wet ingredients into the dry ingredients until you have a moist dough. If you need to, add a tsp of water at a time in order to reach a consistency that feels like playdough.
5. Optional step – you can put the dough in the freezer for half an hour, then roll it out and use cookie cutters. Otherwise, roll the dough into balls, roll the balls in sugar and place on a greased cookie sheet,

about 2 inches apart.

6. Bake at 375 for 8-10 minutes. They will come out of the oven looking as though they aren't done – but they are! Let them cool on the cookie sheet for a minute, then use a spatula to move them to cooling racks for at least 15 minutes for best results.

Note: this procedure makes a nice soft ginger cookie – if you want a crisp ginger snap, roll them out thin and bake for 10-12 minutes.

Chocolate shortbread cookies

Ingredients:

- 1-1/8 cups of flour
- 1 cup of unsweetened cocoa powder
- 1 teaspoon salt
- 1 cup of salted butter, softened or coconut oil with a dash of salt
- 2/3 cup of icing sugar

Directions:

1. Preheat oven to 350F

2. Sift together flour, cocoa, and salt.

3. Using a hand mixer, beat butter or coconut oil and sugar until combined.

4. Pat dough into an **ungreased** pan. The dough won't really hold together and you will think that it needs more moisture – but it doesn't! Trust me!

5. Bake for 20 to 25 minutes. Allow it to cool for 5 minutes, then remove from the pan and cut into squares.

6. Sprinkle with icing sugar and allow the cookies to cool.

Variation:

- Instead of patting the cookie dough into a pan, squeeze together small balls of dough and place them on a cookie sheet.
- Press your thumb into the cookie ball.
- Fill the thumbprint with raspberry jam.
- Bake for 20 minutes.
- Remove from the pan and place on a rack to cool. You can sprinkle the cookie lightly with icing sugar if desired.

How to eat from the pantry when you have no money for groceries

When things go wrong and we have more month than money, it can be difficult to keep the family fed, the bills paid, and a roof over our heads. However, if you have built a well-stocked pantry, you have one less thing to worry about when you have no money for groceries.

Anyone can have a difficult week (or month or year). Maybe an unexpected expense arose, like a trip to the emergency room or a car repair. Perhaps a job was lost or hours were cut at work. It's possible that something happened that made the primary breadwinner for the family unable to work for a time. Whatever the case, having some supplies put back can really help you through a rough spot. While some folks have room in their budgets for these shortfalls or added expenses, a growing number of us are one missed paycheck away from disaster.

The key is this: when times are good, you should focus on loading up your pantry for when times are not so good. It's not a new idea. It's how our ancestors did it because they never knew when a fluke cold snap would kill their crops, when a predator might get the animal they were depending on for food or when a drought would occur.

What you should have in your pantry

Much has been written about the specific items to stock in your pantry, so this is just a general list.

- Dried goods like grains and beans
- Pantry staples like baking supplies
- Meat and produce for the freezer (we won't really talk much about freezer ingredients here)
- Canned goods like meat, soup, fruits, and vegetables
- Powdered milk

The best-case scenario is to store what you already eat. If you generally eat meals with a lot of meat and little plant protein, you're going to feel deprived if you suddenly switch from steak to beans. If you tend to eat lots of protein and vegetables, you're not going to feel your best if you suddenly switch to a diet loaded with starches and high in carbohydrates.

One really good way to see what you're already eating is to write down everything your family consumes for a couple of weeks. You can probably remember most of what you had the past week to give yourself a guideline.

Now, while everything is normal, take a long hard look at your consumption. Are these foods that you can stock up on or do you focus on things that require a couple of trips to the store per week for freshness? If the latter is the case, you might want to make some simple adjustments so that it will be easier to maintain your diet in difficult times.

When some people hear the question, "How long could you survive on the food you have on hand?" they tend to think of the math. "I have 472 servings of grain divided by 4 people and..."

Stop that.

You need to think in terms of *meals*. Those who think in individual components like this are the ones who will end up eating canned peaches, stale saltines, and pureed pumpkin for dinner. Not the most enticing combo, right?

One really great way to stock up and have familiar food on hand is to think about 7 meals that your family enjoys. Then, purchase for your pantry the ingredients for 4 of each of those meals. Here are a few quick tips.

- Look for non-perishable options, like dried or canned mushrooms, onion flakes, bell pepper flakes, and garlic flakes for seasoning meals.
- Learn how to make baked goods from scratch and stock up on the ingredients you need for them.
- Keep fruit and veggies on hand in canned form.
- Have some quick meals on hand so that you don't end up breaking the budget on takeout food on a super busy day.

- Stock up on pasta, rice, quinoa, barley, and other grains, and store them carefully.

Pantry friendly adaptations

Lots of folks say things like, "I only buy fresh XXX at the store – everything else came from the pantry." That's awesome – truly – but if you were in a situation in which you couldn't buy fresh XXX, you probably wouldn't want to go without it, right?

Here are some things to stockpile so that you can make adaptations to fresh XXX

- **Milk**: Powdered milk, canned condensed or evaporated milk.
- **Bread**: Stock up on the ingredients to make it yourself. Store-bought bread is usually loaded with additives, so learning to bake your own is a worthy skill, and it couldn't be easier.
- **Fresh fruit**: Canned fruit is more useful than you might think. You can also use it in smoothies, thaw, and top yogurt or pancakes with it, or bake with it. We are huge applesauce fans, so I can a few dozen jars of this each fall, but you can also buy jars of it at the store. I also make loads of homemade jam which can be used in a multitude of ways that do not

include toast.

- **Salad**: If you have a sunny windowsill, you can grow salad greens all year long to sate your craving for fresh greens. There are lots of delicious microgreen kits on the market, and even some kits that are soil-free. Other alternatives are lightly cooked veggie salads made from freezer vegetables.
- **Vegetables**: You really don't have to have fresh asparagus in February, contrary to what the grocery stores portray. Keep canned veggies in your pantry, and be on the lookout for tasty ways to use them. I also keep dehydrated veggies on hand for cooking with: mushrooms, bell pepper, onion, etc. If you have a root cellar, lots of good veggies can be stored there.

Sample meals from our food storage pantry

Here are some of the meals I've created from my pantry.

- Homemade pancakes topped with fruit syrup made from home-canned jam
- Homemade granola or granola cookies
- Mixed veggie hash – drain a couple of cans of mixed veggies (with potato). Fry them up in some fat with bell pepper and onion (fresh or dehydrated). Serve with eggs if you have them.

- Oatmeal topped with warmed jam
- Homemade bread (or cornbread) and jam
- Smoothies
- Toast with butter or peanut butter
- Roasted veggies topped with parmesan cheese
- Soup and bread
- Refried beans and rice topped with salsa or hot sauce
- Make burritos with canned refried beans and hot sauce.
- Peanut butter and crackers, with some applesauce for dessert
- Tuna and saltines
- Pasta with marinara
- "Risotto" with veggies – cook regular rice in milk (powdered) with canned peas and carrots. Season with garlic, salt, pepper, and Parmesan
- Tuna casserole
- Baked beans with mac and cheese
- Vegetable soup or stew and bread
- Vegetarian chili
- Split pea soup
- Potato soup (it's a family favorite and super-thrifty!)
- Rice pilaf with canned veggies mixed in
- Fried rice with canned veggies
- Noodles with peanut sauce
- Boxed scalloped potatoes, baked beans, and homemade bread

Look at the pantry items you and your family like, then extend those to full meals. You can honestly make some very tasty stuff this way.

What a Crock

I live for the crock pot. I was talking to my daughter about it the other day and we both agreed – it doesn't even feel like you're actually cooking. Plop some stuff into the put in the morning and switch it on. Then go and knit a sweater/go to work/save the world, and by the time you get home, a hot and tasty dinner is ready.

Below are some of my favorite super-duper easy and versatile recipes. A few of them will be featured in the next chapter, Food with a Future.

"Rotisserie" chicken

I love rotisserie chicken but have no rotisserie. (sniff) Imagine how excited I was to learn that I could make my own rotisserie chicken in the crockpot.

If you enjoy eating the skin, you can put the cooked chicken in the oven on broil for a few minutes after it's thoroughly cooked to get it crisp.

It's *so* simple.

Ingredients:

- 1 whole chicken, rinsed and patted dry, innards removed
- 2 tbsp of olive oil
- Seasonings of choice (I use salt, pepper, garlic powder, onion powder, a dash of cayenne, and 1/4 tsp of sugar)
- Onions and/or lemons (optional)

Directions:

1. If you have a roasting rack for your slow cooker, insert it. If you don't, wad up 6 balls of tinfoil for the bottom or slice onions and/or lemons in half. You want to raise your chicken up a little to let the juices run down and steam it. If you don't raise it up, your chicken may be more of a stewed texture from sitting in the juices.
2. Rub the chicken with oil and seasonings.
3. Place the chicken in the crockpot and cook it on low for 6-8 hours. *Do not add any other liquid.* When it's done, it will be tender and practically falling apart in its deliciousness.
4. Because I grew up in the South, gravy is essential in our household. If you, too, are of the gravy persuasion, you can use the drippings and some

flour or cornstarch to make gravy on the stovetop while you brown your chicken in the broiler.

That's it. Easy peasy, lemon squeezy.

Pot roast

You may see the words "pot roast" and go into spasms over the outrageous expense of a beef roast. You can make this with any cut of meat, and actually, the cheaper stuff is usually better for this. (Remember, FAT IS FLAVOR.) I generally use a beef roast for this, but it also works fine with a pork roast.

Also, you can make it without the booze, but alcohol helps to break down the fibers in the meat, making the outcome far more tender. You can store the remainder of your can of beer in the fridge without worrying about it losing its oomph. I mean, I wouldn't want to drink it after a week, but I'd totally use it in another recipe.

Ingredients:

- 1 beef roast (any size that'll fit in your crockpot)
- 1/2 a can of beer
- Beef bouillon cube or powder (optional but delicious)

- 2 glugs of Worcestershire sauce
- 2 onions, cut in quarters
- 4 cloves of garlic, smashed
- Carrots, cut into chunks
- Potatoes cut into chunks
- 1 tsp of paprika powder
- 1 tsp of thyme leaves
- Salt and pepper to taste

Later you'll need 2 tbsp of flour and 1 tbsp of butter to make gravy from the cooking liquid.

Directions:

1. Some folks like to brown the roast in oil before putting it in the crock pot. If you have time, it's quite nice, but if you are in a rush, it will still be delicious if you don't.
2. Pour beer, bouillon Worcestershire sauce, and seasonings into the crockpot and stir them up.
3. Add the veggies and the roast.
4. Put the lid on and cook on high for 6 hours or low for 8-10 hours.
5. When the roast is done, remove it and the veggies to a plate. In a saucepan, melt your butter and whisk in the flour to make a thick roux. Stir in the liquid from the roast, whisking continuously. Season this with

more salt and pepper if needed. I like to add some parsley because it's pretty, but it doesn't add much flavor.

Serve the roast with gravy.

Salsa chicken

This can barely even be called a recipe – it's that easy! My daughter always loved this dish and thought it must be super-complicated. She was stunned when I told her what was in it.

Ingredients:

- 2 pounds of boneless skinless chicken (thighs or breasts)
- 1 jar of salsa (cheap salsa is perfectly fine)

Directions:

1. Put your salsa in the crockpot
2. Put your chicken in the crockpot.
3. Cook it on high for 6 hours.
4. Take the chicken out and shred it with two forks.

5. Put it back in for another hour.

Boom. Done.

Fruity pork (or chicken)

I make loads of jam every single year with whatever fruit I have on hand or whatever I can get cheap. Stone fruit jams seem to work best for this, such as plum, peach, and apricot. You can also use orange marmalade. If you prefer, you could use skinless, boneless chicken, or even chicken quarters.

Ingredients:

- 2-3 pounds of boneless pork – you can use loin, tenderloin shoulder, or pork chops
- 1 cup of jam
- 3 tbsp of soy sauce
- 4 cloves of garlic minced
- 1/2 an onion minced

Directions:

1. Mix jam and soy sauce together in the crock pot.

2. Add pork, garlic, and onion.
3. Cook on high for 5 hours or low for 8.
4. When the meat is falling apart, it's ready to eat.

Serve this over rice with a steamed veggie. I really like it with green beans or broccoli.

Chili

I swear I should have a whole chapter just for chili. I flippin' love it and it's kind of my specialty. Any time someone is coming over and I ask what they want, it's chili. As it is, I'll share with you 4 different chilis that you may enjoy.

Here's the basic version.

Ingredients:

- 1 pound of ground whatever (beef, chicken, turkey, pork)
- 1 can of crushed tomatoes
- 1 can of pinto beans, undrained
- 1 can of kidney beans, undrained
- 1 diced onion
- 1/2 diced bell pepper

- 4 cloves of garlic, crushed
- 1/2 a can of beer
- 3 tbsp of chili powder
- 1 tsp of cumin
- Beef bouillon cube or powder (optional but delicious)
- salt and pepper to taste
- Optional: finely diced jalapenos or crushed red chili peppers to add some heat

Directions:

1. Y'all, you don't even need to cook the meat first. Just dump it into the crock pot.
2. Add all the other ingredients.
3. Cook it on low for 8 hours.

Serve it with crackers, fresh bread, or cornbread. Top it with shredded cheddar cheese. (Actually, we "bottom" it with cheese – then the cheese is melted by the piping hot chili.)

Sweet and spicy chili

This is pretty similar to the standard chili with a couple of delicious differences. If you leave out the spicy stuff, children generally enjoy this chili.

Ingredients:

- 1 pound of ground whatever (beef, chicken, turkey, pork)
- 1 can of crushed tomatoes
- 2 cans of baked beans, undrained
- 1/2 cup of barbecue sauce – our favorite is Sweet Baby Ray's
- 1 diced onion
- 1/2 diced bell pepper
- 4 cloves of garlic, crushed
- 3 tbsp of chili powder
- 1 tsp of cumin
- 1 tbsp of brown sugar
- 1/2 tsp of cayenne pepper
- salt and pepper to taste
- Optional: finely diced jalapenos or crushed red chili peppers to add some heat

Directions:

1. Mix crushed tomatoes, barbecue sauce, and spices together.
2. Add all the other ingredients.
3. Cook it on low for 8 hours.

Vegetarian chili

Got some vegetarians or vegans in your life? Even hardcore carnivores will love this chili. And bonus – it's DIRT CHEAP.

Ingredients:

- 1 can of crushed tomatoes
- 1 can of pinto beans, undrained
- 1 can of kidney beans, undrained
- 1 can of black beans
- 1 can of whole-kernel corn
- 1 diced onion
- 1/2 diced bell pepper
- 4 cloves of garlic, crushed
- 3 tbsp of chili powder
- 1 tsp of cumin

- salt and pepper to taste
- Optional: finely diced jalapenos or crushed red chili peppers to add some heat

Directions:

1. Dump every single thing into the crockpot
2. Cook it on low for 4-6 hours.

Southwestern white chicken chili

You could technically call this stew if you're trying to act like we make something besides chili.

Ingredients:

- 1 pound of boneless skinless poultry (you can also use ground chicken or turkey)
- 1 can of chicken broth
- 2 cans of white kidney beans or cannelloni beans, undrained
- 1 diced onion
- 1/2 diced bell pepper (I like to use yellow for this one)

- 4 cloves of garlic, crushed
- 1/2 a can of beer
- 3 tbsp of chili powder
- 1 tsp of cumin
- salt and pepper to taste
- Optional: finely diced jalapenos or crushed red chili peppers to add some heat

Directions:

1. Mix broth, beer, and seasonings in the crockpot.
2. Add the meat
3. Add all the other ingredients.
4. Cook it on high for 6 hours or low for 8 hours.

Stroganoff

This is a meal my kiddos ask me to make for special occasions. It's actually pretty versatile, allowing you to use your choice of what's on sale.

Ingredients:

- 1 pound of stewing beef (or ground beef)

- 1 cup of broth (beef or vegetable), wine, or beer
- 1 cup of sliced mushrooms
- 1/2 an onion, finely minced
- 1 tbsp of butter for now and 1 tbsp of butter for later
- 1 tablespoon Worcestershire sauce
- 1 tsp or garlic powder
- salt and pepper to taste
- 1 cup of cream cheese, sour cream, or plain yogurt
- 1 tbsp of flour or cornstarch

Directions:

1. In a skillet, melt the butter and saute the mushrooms and onions until they're brown and fragrant.
2. Scrape all the veggies and oil into the crockpot.
3. Add meat, broth, Worcestershire sauce, garlic powder, salt, and pepper.
4. Cook it in the crockpot on low for 7 hours.
5. In a skillet, whisk flour or cornstarch into melted butter to make a roux.
6. Scoop out as much cooking liquid as possible and whisk it into the roux, then pour the whole thing back into the crockpot.
7. Cook it for another hour on high to let the sauce thicken.
8. Add a cup of cream cheese, sour cream, or plain

yogurt and stir it well. Let it cook for 10 more minutes to heat through.

Serve this over wide egg noodles, gnocchi, or rice. My dad used to like the leftover sauce over toast.

Food with a Future

Sometimes I make a meal and say to it, "Sunshine, you've got a bright future ahead of you."

Actually, no, I don't really talk to my food using my outside voice. But I think it.

There are some foods you make and you know you're going to have leftovers. Most folks don't like to eat the Exact Same Meal every day for a week, but with our tips, you can sneakily give your family just that, and they'll never know it. This, my friends, is Food with a Future. A future as other delectable meals to which nobody will turn up a snooty little nose.

When I was a working mom, this was one of my biggest time savers. I'd make a big batch of whatever, then reinvent it throughout the week to rounds of applause and standing ovations. Okay, nobody actually clapped, but they really liked it.

Roasted, rotisserie, or salsa chicken

There's so much you can do with leftover chicken! I like to shred whatever is left and use it in various concoctions. First, let's look at a plainer chicken. (All of these things will also work with turkey or other poultry.)

Make broth

Once you've gotten the bigger part of the meat off the chicken, use the carcass to make a rich and tasty broth. I like to use the crockpot for this. Plop all the bones, the meat you may not wish to eat, giblets, and skin into the pot, along with 6-8 cups of water. I like to add six cloves of smashed garlic, some celery, and a couple of onions to the mix. You can also add salt and pepper, but I generally wait until the end to see how salty it turns out from the skin.

Cook the broth on low for 8-12 hours. I usually let it go overnight. Then let it cool enough, so you don't burn yourself from the steam. Place a large colander over a pot, then pour the broth through to strain out the bones, gristle, skin, and overcooked vegetables. Allow everything to cool in the fridge, including the stuff in the strainer. Then, pick any meat off the bones that would be a tasty addition to your future soup and add it to the broth. Go through the contents of your colander and grab any meat that has fallen off the carcass during the cooking process and add that to your broth as well. Season it as desired.

This broth can be used right away for soup or frozen in ziplock freezer bags for later use. If you like canning, you can also put it back in shelf-stable fashion with your pressure canner.

BBQ chicken pizza

Spread your favorite barbecue sauce on the pizza shell of your choice. Top it with chicken, mushrooms, onions, bell peppers, and hot peppers (or whatever toppings you like). Then sprinkle shredded cheese on top and bake as directed.

Chicken noodle soup

Use your tasty broth for a base. Add a can of peas and carrots and the noodles of your choice. Bring it to a boil until the noodles are cooked to your liking. Serve immediately.

Chicken and dumplings

Here's my daughter's dumpling recipe.

You need about a cup of flour, cold water (as needed), 1 tsp of salt, and 2 tbsp melted butter for this one.

1. Add your flour and salt into a bowl, and slowly add cold water, about 1 tbsp. at a time. You want it to be a very dense and firm mix.
2. Once your flour, water, and salt are thoroughly combined, break it into pieces and pour the melted butter over, and knead everything together until it's smooth. If it's feeling sticky, you'll want to add more flour to it.
3. Let it rest for about 10-20 minutes under a warm damp cloth.
4. Once the time is up, you're going to take little chunks (about the size of a Brussels sprout) out of your dough, and roll it out into a long strip on a floured surface.

Finished! Once your dough is done, you can throw the strips of dough into the broth, cook for about 15 minutes, and enjoy! They'll float to the top when they're finished cooking. Dumplings can add a really nice texture to your soups or stews, and make you feel full for a little bit longer.

I like to add chives and black pepper to my dumpling dough for some added flavor.

Chicken pot pie

Use some of your broth to make a white gravy. Stir in a drained can of mixed veggies and 1-2 cups of shredded chicken. Put it all into a cast iron skillet or another oven-proof dish, then top it with a pie crust. (Either make your own or use a storebought one. Bake it in the oven as directed for the crust and let it rest for 5 minutes to thicken. Serve immediately.

Thai chicken slaw

This is one of my all-time fave throw-togethers. You can cut up your own cabbage or you can buy a coleslaw mix from the store.

Here's what you need:

- 1/2 cup of shredded chicken per person
- Shredded cabbage
- Optional: shredded carrots, chopped green onion, chopped fresh cilantro, finely sliced bell pepper, shredded radish, chopped peanuts

- Crunchy chow mein noodles for topping

Peanut sauce

Whatever you do, for the love of Thailand, don't leave out the cumin. That's the secret ingredient I coaxed out of the chef at our favorite Thai restaurant in Virginia.

Ingredients:

- 1/3 cup of peanut butter (smooth or crunchy)
- ½ cup of broth or water
- 1 tbsp of soy sauce
- 1 tbsp of rice vinegar (or white vinegar)
- 1 tbsp of garlic powder
- 1 tsp of cumin
- 1 tsp of ginger powder
- 1 tsp of sugar or honey
- Optional: Crushed red chili pepper flakes

Directions:

1. In a cooking pot, add peanut butter, soy sauce, rice vinegar, garlic powder, ginger powder, cumin, and broth or water.

2. Warm this up on low heat and whisk constantly.
3. When the sauce is smooth and creamy, add the sugar or honey and whisk for another minute.
4. Remove from heat.

You can alternatively make this sauce in a food processor.

For the slaw:

Toss all the ingredients together in a large bowl and dress with peanut sauce. Toss it well and eat it immediately.

Chicken rice casserole

Comfort food with a capital C. Use the formula in Chapter 2 to make this your very own. I like to use shredded chicken, cooked brown rice, a creamy bechamel sauce, some shredded cheddar, and cauliflower. Mix it up with your faves. Bake it for 45 minutes at 375F.

Chicken salad

Another super easy use – I have two different recipes. First, there's the typical chicken salad with mayo, chopped red onion, salt, a dash of mustard powder, and black pepper.

The other is the "fancy" version. Mix up shredded chicken, green onion, and red grapes with poppy seed dressing. It's incredible!

Taco salad

My daughter uses leftover salsa chicken, onions, bell peppers, leftover rice and beans, and lettuce. For the dressing, she mixes about ⅓ cup of ranch, your basic taco seasonings, and some of the juice from the salsa chicken. She also fries up some strips of tortillas with a spritz of lime juice and salt to mix into the salad. Who doesn't love a good crunch?

Empanadas

This one is straight from my daughter.

With the last little bit of salsa chicken, I like to make empanadas. They're not too much effort, but more than the above meals, and they're so freaking tasty. I typically do a mix of chicken empanadas and veggie ones.

Here's how I make them:

- Pie crust
- Chicken
- Cheese
- Veggies (I'll use some of the frozen veggie blend, bell peppers, and onions)
- Potatoes
- Beans

Take two small potatoes, and chop them up pretty small. Boil them until just before they're fork tender. Chop up your onions and peppers, and add any leftover juice from the salsa chicken into a pan. Once those are cooked, I take half out and set them to the side. Add the frozen veggies, potatoes, and beans. It's around here where I'll add some seasoning.

Once everything is cooked and has a good flavor to it, I prepare the dough. Take your premade pie crust out, and grab about a golf ball size chunk off. Roll it into a circle that's about ¼ inch thick, and 5-ish inches in diameter. Preheat the oven to 400F, and get ready to make your empanadas.

Mix the onions and peppers you'd put to the side with the leftover salsa chicken, and grab your other filling as well. Put a generous scoop (probably about 2 tbsp) in the center of the dough, you can sprinkle a little bit of cheese on here, but that's completely optional. Fold the dough over, so it's in a half-circle shape, and pinch the edges together. You can use your fingers or a fork for this. Pop an egg wash over the top, and throw those bad boys in the oven for about 20 minutes or until golden brown. If you don't finish all of them, they freeze very well too, but for me, they typically won't last that long.

Pot roast

Carnivore that I am, I positively adore pot roast in all its various forms. Here are some of the ways I use the leftovers:

Beef stew

Use your leftover meat and veggies for a tasty stew. Chop everything into bite-sized pieces. Add 1-2 cups of beef broth to your gravy and stir it well. Then add in your leftover meat and vegetables, plus one can each of green peas and carrots. Simmer it for 15-20 minutes until the sauce is thickened. Serve it with fresh, crusty bread.

Enchiladas

Toss your shredded meat with some chili powder and tomato paste. Add a can of drained black beans if you need to make it go further. Roll it into tortillas, then pour a can of your favorite enchilada sauce over it. Cover it with foil and bake it for 40 minutes at 375F. Remove the foil and top it with shredded cheese. Cook it for another 5 minutes, then let it rest for 10 before serving.

Fruity pork

I love that fruity pork with every fiber of my being, and it makes tasty leftovers!

Pork pilaf

Cook some rice in chicken broth. Add in chopped pork and some of the leftover sauce. I like to add slivered almonds and craisins or raisins to this. It's Morrocan-ish. This is also tasty with cooked quinoa instead of rice.

Spring roll bowl

You could turn this into spring rolls if you are more industrious than me. I, however, and far too lazy for the rolling and such, so I make this into a bowl. Be fancy. Say it's "deconstructed." Stir fry some cabbage, onion, and chopped pork or chicken with soy sauce. Pop it in a bowl and top it with crumbled, fried spring roll wrappers. Alternatively, crumble crunchy chow mein noodles on top. Boom. Done.

BBQ

The sweetness of the fruity sauce goes really well with barbecue. Shred your meat (chicken or pork) and toss it with barbecue sauce and a splash of white vinegar. Serve it on toasted buns with a slice of coleslaw.

Vietnamese noodle salad

Cook some vermicelli noodles with boiling water. Toss them with shredded pork or chicken, green onions, cucumber, drained and chopped pineapple rings, and cilantro if you have it. Mix the reserved pineapple juice with a splash of white vinegar or rice wine vinegar, soy sauce, and a teaspoon of sugar. Drizzle the dressing over your salad and serve immediately.

Chili

I love chili. Not only does it taste absolutely delicious, it's also a relatively frugal meal. (You can make it more or less thrifty with your ingredients.) I have several different meals I make with leftover chili that can help you to extend the batch past the "bowl of chili" phase.

We usually eat it at least twice as just a "bowl of chili" and then, depending how much is left, I turn to one or more of the following recipes to use up the rest of it. You can make the following dishes with a hearty meaty chili, a vegetarian chili, or even canned chili if you like that.

Chili mac

You can make this hearty, filling dish in a few different ways. The least expensive way is to use a box of macaroni and cheese. Prepare the mac and cheese like you normally would, then stir in your leftover chili. Heat it through and serve it with some crusty bread. My kids loved this when we were uberbroke and couldn't really afford cheese.

If you want to make a better quality version of this, simply cook your pasta – I prefer shells or macaroni – until it's al dente. Stir in your leftover chili and heat it through. Then, before it's done, dump in about a cup of shredded extra-sharp cheddar cheese. I like to top it with some sour cream and diced green onion.

Chili pie

This is also an old favorite, and there are two ways to make it – from scratch or with a mix.

- To make chili pie, grease an oven-safe casserole dish or pie pan and fill the bottom of it with thick, leftover chili.
- Add a layer of cheese (or skip the cheese – it's good either way).
- Top that with drained, canned corn or frozen corn.
- Now for the good part – cover it with cornbread batter. I have loved Jiffy cornbread mix since I was a little girl. Don't judge. It's super easy to make and has just the right amount of sweetness. You can top it with Jiffy batter or make your own cornbread batter from scratch. Layer that directly on top of the

corn.

Bake it as per the instructions for your cornbread, until you can poke it with a knife and have it come out clean. Allow the chili pie to sit for 10 minutes before slicing and serving.

Chili dogs

This hardly needs directions, but here goes.

Cook hotdogs in your favorite way. Toast some hot dog buns. Lay the cooked dogs in the buns, then top it with chili, chopped white onion, and cheese. DONE.

Chili burritos

My dad love-love-loved a burrito with chili. It was often the birthday meal he asked for. Naturally, on his birthday every year, I make them in his honor.

- Make a homemade burrito in whatever way you normally do. I like them with ground beef and refried beans as the filling.
- Heat up your leftover chili. Spoon it on top of your burrito and then either sprinkle grated cheese on

top or ladle some cheese sauce over it.

Eat this messy delicious beast with a knife and fork.

Nachos

The absolute easiest way to make nachos, in my opinion, is with leftover chili. I use my cast iron skillet for this.

- Layer a big pile of tortilla chips in the bottom of the skillet.
- Top it with pre-heated chili. (I always heat the chili first because it needs longer to heat up than the chips require in the oven.)
- Top that with either shredded cheese or cheese sauce.
- Top that with some pickled jalapenos, bell peppers, onions, olives, and/or tomatoes.

Serve it with sour cream, salsa, and/or guacamole.

You can also make a kid-friendly version if you have a mega-muffin tin. Each muffin area contains the chips, chili and cheese, along with any toppings your child likes. I only use the big muffin tin for this as the smaller ones are simply too small.

I hope this gets your wheels turning

Think about other foods that you make which leave tons of leftovers behind. Would any of these recipes apply to your leftovers? It's so much easier to get your family to eat leftovers when they're disguised as something totally new!

Love Your Leftovers

In these times of budget cuts, rising food costs, job losses, and ever-increasing expenses, we can't afford to let anything go to waste. In fact, it isn't far-fetched to consider this our practice run for the tough days that may be ahead.

One way to stretch your food budget is with the humble leftover.

Have you ever been really poor? I don't mean "I can't afford Starbucks until my next paycheck" poor. I mean "Should I buy food or pay the electric bill before the power gets shut off" poor.

I have absolutely been that poor back when my oldest daughter was a baby. When you are that broke, every single bite of food in the house counts. You cannot afford to let anything go to waste. Following are some ideas to help you make use of anything you happen to have left over.

Menage a Leftover

This is where the "Menage a Leftover" bucket in the freezer comes in.

In our freezer, we kept an empty ice cream tub. After each meal, those tiny amounts of food that don't add up to a full serving got popped into the bucket. And because of our situation, I often would take food that was uneaten on a family member's plate to add to the bucket. Desperate times, desperate measures. What people might consider "gross" in good times, they would feel lucky to have in bad times. Then, usually about once per week, the contents of that bucket in the freezer were turned into a meal.

I drew some criticism from friends and relatives during that time for the distance I went not to waste a single bite of food. A few people commented that it was ridiculous, and others thought combining all those different foods in the freezer was disgusting. One person even referred to the meals as "garbage disposal meals." It stung a little at the time, but looking back, I'm glad to have had that experience. I can draw upon it if times become difficult in the future. While other people are trying to figure out where their next meal is coming from, I *know* that I can take the same amount of groceries and make at least two more meals out of them.

I always considered meals from the leftover bucket to be "free food" because they were perfectly serviceable items that you'd normally throw out. So, let's say, you have a little bit of broccoli, some mashed potatoes, some beef gravy, a scoop of ground beef, some corn...you know? The remains of meals. What can you do with that?

This is where being creative with the spices comes in. I might take the above, add a can of beans and a tin of tomato paste, and turn it into a chili-flavored soup. Alternatively, I could stir in some yogurt and some noodles and make it into a creamy casserole, well-seasoned with thyme. I could sprinkle a bit of cheese on it, wrap it in pie crust and make turnovers. The trick is to make something totally new and different from it so that it doesn't even seem like leftovers. Some of the concoctions were absolutely delicious – so good that we recreated them with fresh ingredients later on. Others were not-so-great. Only a couple of times did we end up with something that was really awful.

If you can serve your family one "freebie" meal per week, that results in a savings, for a family of 4 of about $10, or $520 over the course of a year. It doesn't sound like much until you add it up, does it?

We don't always do the leftover bucket these days because times are not as tight as they were back then. However, we do creatively use our leftovers.

Leftover buffet

Leftover Buffet Night is something my girls always looked forward to each week. My oldest daughter used to say it was "just like going to Golden Corral." I have my doubts that it's Golden Corral level, but hey, it made her happy without the $20 price tag.

What's Leftover Buffet Night?

Simply put, all the items from the fridge are placed on the counter. We have some nice little oven-safe dishes that are divided. Everyone takes their divided dish and helps themselves to whatever leftovers they'd like for dinner. The dish is then placed in the oven and heated up – sort of like a "TV dinner" of choice.

Aside from the kids scrapping it out over the last enchilada, this is generally very successful, and there's rarely anything left. Anything that is left goes into the Menage a Leftover bucket or gets frozen as a single serving.

Soup

When I don't have quite enough to make two full servings, but it's a bit more than one serving, I often make soup.

I can or freeze broth on a regular basis, so it's an easy thing to grab a jar of broth, chop up the meat, add some vegetables, and stir in a starch. You can stretch your soup by adding barley, pasta, potatoes, or rice. If you have fresh bread to serve with it and a little sprinkle of Parmesan or cheddar for the top, you have a hot, comforting meal for pennies.

Puree

Puree can be a side dish or a soup.

I use this technique quite often with leftover root veggies. Using a food processor, puree potatoes, carrots, turnips, parsnips, or other root vegetables. You can add milk, broth, or even water to thin the puree to the consistency of mashed potatoes or soup, depending on how you intend to use it.

Season this with garlic powder, onion powder, and other appropriate spices. Then garnish it with a tiny amount of bacon, chives, cheese, or sour cream.

Other vegetables that are suited for puree are cauliflower, broccoli, and squash.

Pie

This is a great way to use up leftover meat and gravy. In the bottom of a pie pan or cast iron skillet, stir meat that has been cut into bite-sized pieces with gravy. If you don't have leftover gravy, a creamy soup, a bechamel sauce, or a thickened broth will work. Add in complimentary vegetables, also in bite-sized pieces. We like peas, corn, and carrots with poultry, and green beans, carrots, and potatoes with beef. Add seasoning if needed.

Top your pie with either a standard pie crust, cornbread batter, or with biscuit dough topping. (2 recipes below) Bake as directed, then allow it to cool for about 5 minutes before serving.

For even smaller amounts of leftovers (or picky eaters), you can use individual-sized ovenproof containers or ramekins to make single-serving "pies."

I've also used muffin tins designed for the jumbo muffins to make individual pies. When using a muffin tin, you will want to make it a two-crust pie to enclose the filling.

Pockets

If I bake it in a pocket, my kids will eat it. Whether the filling is savory or sweet, there's something about a piping hot turnover that makes anything delicious.

The key with a pocket is that the filling cannot be too runny. So, for a savory pocket, you can mix a small amount of gravy, tomato sauce, or cheese sauce with your meat and/or veggies, but you don't want it to ooze all over the place as soon as someone takes a bite. If you want to eat this as handheld food, allow it to cool for at least 15 minutes before eating it.

You can use pie crust or pizza dough for your pockets. Pizza dough is our personal favorite because it is a bit more filling. I make pockets and keep them in the freezer. I take them out the night before and place them in the refrigerator – by noon, the pocket is thawed and makes a delicious lunch-box treat at school.

We like pockets with veggies and cheese sauce; meat, mushrooms, and gravy; meat and bbq sauce; pizza toppings, marinara, and cheese; and meat and cheese. Another favorite is empanada style: meat flavored with Mexican spices, mixed with salsa, beans, and cheese. As well, you can fill pockets with chopped fruit that is topped with either cream cheese or syrup for a dessert-style turnover. (Drained canned fruit works well for this too.)

Casseroles

The fact is, you can mix nearly anything with a creamy sauce and top it with a crispy topping, and you have a tasty down-home casserole. A basic casserole consists of pre-cooked meat, a veggie, a sauce, a grain, and a topping. Bake at approximately 350F for 30-45 minutes until bubbly and the top is browned. The less meat and veggies you have, the more cooked grains you should add. Try barley, quinoa, rice, pasta, or wheatberries to stretch your casserole. Instant comfort! For toppings, you can use stale bread that has been finely chopped in the food processor, cheese, crumbled crackers, crumbled cereal, or wheat germ, just to name a few items. I often use things that have perhaps become a bit stale – just another way to use up food that would otherwise be discarded.

For more details, revisit The Ultimate Frugal Casserole Formula in Chapter 2.

Be creative!

You're only limited by your imagination when it comes to turning your leftovers into delicious, tasty new meals. Think about your family's favorite dishes. For us, it is anything in a pocket, pot pies and creamy soups. Therefore, when repurposing my leftovers, I try to frequently gear the meals towards those types of foods. A hint of familiarity makes the meal more easily accepted by those you are feeding.

Scalloped potatoes à la leftover

Scalloped potatoes are a holiday staple for many families, but this filling dish has the potential to go so much further than the festive feast. For years, I've used scalloped potatoes as a delicious leftover catch-all.

The lovely thing about scalloped potatoes is that it doesn't have to be an expensive dish or a huge quantity (unless you want them to be.) It's always savory and filling, and the leftovers are potentially even better than the original meal.

I love finding new ways to re-imagine leftovers because using up your leftovers can stretch your food budget like nothing else. Scalloped potato a la leftover is no different.

A little à la leftover inspiration

I made a 2-person Scalloped Potato à la Leftover the other night, and it reminded me that I needed to share the "recipe" with you. As always, I use the term recipe loosely because this is really just a conglomeration of delicious things you have kicking around in the quantity you desire.

My most recent dish consisted of three large potatoes, some onion, some garlic, some oat milk, leftover bratwurst sausage crumbles, and some cauliflower that needed to be used up. I topped it with bread crumbs, baked it at 350F, and It was so tasty and delicious!

I've also made a breakfast-y version with bell peppers and bacon that was a huge morning score!

How to make scalloped potatoes à la leftover

Here's a step-by-step for making your own leftover concoction on a dime. If you leave out the meat and use dairy-free milk, then this recipe can be vegan.

Cut up your potatoes, onions, and garlic

I like to make super-thin slices of potatoes and onion and then dice up my garlic finely. But you do you, Boo. You can cut these things up in basically any way you want as long as the potato pieces are uniform.

Choose a meat (optional)

I use already-cooked, leftover protein for this dish. Some of the things I've used:

- Diced ham
- Ground beef
- Bratwurst or other sausage crumbles
- Chopped spicy salami
- Shredded chicken (your own or rotisserie from the store)

- Smoked turkey from the deli
- Pot roast
- Cooked, crumbled bacon

Prep your veggies

I usually use either leftover veggies in this without an overpowering flavor – like the above-mentioned cauliflower – or root veggies.

- Chop up any leftover veggies to add to your layers.
- Slice any root vegetables to match the slices of potato. Some root veggie options might be carrots, turnips, rutabaga, or parsnips.

Gather your seasonings

I almost always use a combination of the following herbs, but your ingredients will determine your choices.

- Salt
- Black pepper
- Thyme
- Chives
- teeny tiny sprinkle of nutmeg – only a little bitty bit adds a huge amount of richness to the dish.

Select your milk

You can use a variety of different kinds of milk for this dish. My two favorites are:

- Cow's milk
- Oat milk

If money is really tight, try this hack. Boil a small potato in water until it's basically falling apart. Then pop it, water and all, into the blender with a small amount of milk to make the milk go further without just using plain old water.

Now it's time to build your dish

Drum roll...now comes the fun part.

1. Preheat your oven to 350F and assemble your scalloped potatoes a la leftover.
2. Grease your baking dish – I generally use butter, but you can also use cooking oil or shortening.
3. Layer your ingredients, sprinkling all the seasonings but the nutmeg on each layer. Potatoes, onions, other veggies, meat, potatoes, onions, other veggies, meat, repeat. Always end with potatoes.
4. Mix the nutmeg in the milk.

5. Pour milk over the entire dish until you can just see it appearing at the sides of your concoction. I don't usually cover the top layer, but nothing bad will happen if you do.
6. Top the whole shebang with foil and pop it in the oven for 40 minutes.

Check to see if it's done. You'll know because the potatoes and other veggies will be fork-tender.

Top it with goodies

If you want to make it even better, add a topping. Some ideas are:

- Cheese
- Bread crumbs
- Cracker crumbs
- Croutons
- Stuffing mix (it makes a delightful topping, really!)

You can also just take the foil off and add a wee bit of butter to the top and let it get brown.

Cook it for another ten minutes or so, and you're done.

And that's all there is to it!

Let it stand for 5-10 minutes before serving, so it thickens up nicely. Serve this with some steamed veggies or a salad for a balanced, inexpensive meal. If you are full-on pro-carb like me, add some crusty bread to the side.

Seasonal Savings

'Tis the season...for whatever's in season.

It's easy to say for someone to recommend that we all eat "seasonally," but when the food comes in an unfamiliar form or it's an ingredient we haven't tried (at least in its fresh version), it can be a lot easier to slide back into familiar habits.

But you can't overlook the benefits of eating a diet that is more in tune with nature. Not only does it provide you with the nutrients you need at certain times of the year, but it's also MUCH easier on your wallet because of good old supply and demand. Whether you grow a garden or buy from the farmer's market, fill up on a dime with fresh, delicious produce.

This chapter could be an entire book. (And it is – mine's called *The Seasonal Kitchen Companion*, and there are many others.) But for the purposes of this book, we'll do a quick overview with some special tips for each season.

Spring

Let's start off with what is in season during the spring:

- Apricots
- Asparagus
- Beets
- Broccoli
- Cabbage
- Garlic
- Green Beans
- Lettuce
- Mangos
- Mushrooms
- Onions and Leeks
- Peas
- Potatoes, baby
- Radishes
- Rhubarb
- Spinach
- Strawberries

It depends on where you live when and how long these things will be in season. These are all items that like cool weather and sunny afternoons.

The more delicate spring veggies are best when steamed lightly and topped with butter. Asparagus and peas are best with a very gentle and simple treatment. Sweet spring lettuce makes some of the most delicious salads of the year. To make your meals more hearty, there are a few things like beets, broccoli, and potatoes making their last appearance until autumn.

Green pea soup

Ingredients:

- ½ cup chopped onion
- 1 tbsp of butter
- 2 cups of chicken or veggie broth
- 2 cups freshly shelled peas (or 2 packages of frozen peas)
- Black pepper and salt to taste
- 1/4 cup half and half

Directions:

1. In a saucepan, sauté the chopped onion in butter for 5 minutes or until tender.
2. Add the broth and bring it to a boil.
3. Pour in the fresh peas and cook until they're tender, about 3 minutes.

4. Turn off the heat and add salt and pepper.
5. Puree the soup in batches in your blender or food processor.
6. Pour it back into the saucepan, then stir in the cream. Heat gently until the soup is warmed through.
7. Garnish with a few fresh peas and some sour cream. You can also use some fresh herbs like dill, chives, or mint to season the soup.

I usually serve this soup with fresh sourdough bread.

Summer

Here are the things you should be eating during the hot days of summer. Many of them don't require a lick of cooking, and others can be cooked outside on the grill.

- Basil
- Bell Peppers
- Black-eyed Peas
- Blackberries
- Blueberries
- Cantaloupe
- Cherries
- Corn

- Cucumber
- Eggplant
- Grapefruit
- Grapes
- Green Beans
- Honeydew Melon
- Kiwi
- Lima Beans
- Mushrooms
- Peaches
- Plums
- Raspberries
- Summer Squash
- Tomatoes
- Watermelon
- Zucchini

Zucchini fritters

Ingredients:

- 2 cups of coarsely shredded zucchini
- 1 cup of shredded cheddar cheese
- 1 cup of whole wheat flour
- 2 tsp of garlic powder
- 2 tsp of onion powder

- 2 tsp of MSG-free seasoning salt
- fresh ground black pepper to taste
- 1/8 cup of cooking oil

Directions:

1. In a large bowl, mix together flour and seasonings.
2. Stir in zucchini and cheese, using your hands to combine well.
3. Meanwhile, heat the cooking oil until it sizzles when a drop of water is added.
4. Form the zucchini mixture into patties and place them in the hot oil, taking care not to splatter yourself.
5. Fry on each side for about 3-4 minutes or until a dark golden brown.
6. Drain the fritters on a paper towel.
7. Serve with sour cream or yogurt garlic dip.

Baked variation:

1. Form the zucchini fritters as instructed above. 2. Preheat the oven to 400F
2. Lightly oil a cookie sheet.
3. Place the fritters on the cookie sheet and brush them lightly with oil.

4. Bake for approximately 10 minutes on each side or until dark golden brown.

Garlic green beans

Ingredients:

- 1 pound of washed, trimmed green beans
- 3 cloves of fresh garlic, finely minced
- 2 tbsp of cooking oil
- Soy sauce to taste (if you don't do soy sauce, you can use Bragg's Coconut Amino instead)
- 1-2 tablespoons of honey

Directions:

1. In a skillet over medium heat, warm the cooking oil until a drop of water splashed on it sizzles. Add the fresh garlic and stir it until it's golden and fragrant.
2. Meanwhile, lightly steam your green beans until they're a vivid green, but not thoroughly cooked.
3. Turn up the heat on the skillet, and add the drained green beans, stirring frequently. Cook for 3-5 minutes, until the beans have reached the desired tenderness.

4. Sprinkle the beans with soy sauce and stir in the honey. Keeping the skillet on high heat, stir the beans constantly until they are caramelized.
5. Serve immediately.

Homemade fuzzy peach candy

If you're going to be processing lots of peaches, SAVE THE PEELS. This is a delicious use for them. Obviously, wash the peaches well before peeling them.

Ingredients:

- Peach peels
- Lemon juice
- Turbinado or "raw" sugar (the crunchy crystals are way nicer for this than a finer sugar)

Directions:

1. Place all of your peels in a large bowl. Add lemon juice based on the amount of peels you have. I had peels from 20 pounds worth of peaches and used 1/8 cup of lemon juice. Toss peels in juice.
2. In another bowl, put a little bit of turbinado sugar.

3. Toss a large spoonful of peach peels in the sugar and then place them in a single layer on the tray of a dehydrator. (Use a liner for the tray. Dehydrated sugar doesn't come off easily.) Continue until all of the peels have been tossed with the sugar.

Dehydrate at 135F for 6-8 hours. Store in an airtight container.

How to make sunflower seed pesto

Do you have more basil than you know what to do with? What better way to celebrate basil season than to make fresh pesto! That potent, garlicky sauce is the bedrock of many quick, simple meals.

Not only is it delicious, but it's loaded with nutrients and antioxidants! Pesto contains vitamins A, K, and E, as well as calcium, iron, and essential fatty acids.

The only problem is that unless you happen to have a free or cheap source of pine nuts, they are outrageously expensive.

You can solve that problem using the humble, thrifty sunflower seed. Heck, if you grow sunflowers, you can find pretty much every single ingredient for this in your backyard garden. You may even find that Sunflower Seed

Pesto is your new favorite condiment and forget that pine nuts ever even existed in pesto.

Ingredients:

- 2 cups of fresh basil
- 1/3 cup of roasted sunflower seeds
- 4-6 cloves of garlic
- 1/2 cup of grated Parmesan cheese
- 1/2 cup of olive oil

Directions:

1. Coarsely grind roasted sunflower seeds in a food processor – don't turn them into powder! If the seeds are salted, that's okay – just don't add salt to the pesto.
2. Wash the basil leaves and then pat them dry gently. Avoid getting too much stem.
3. In the food processor, pulse the sunflower seeds and cloves of garlic. Then add the basil, grated Parmesan cheese, and olive oil and pulse until it is the consistency that you desire.
4. Stir pesto into hot pasta for a fresh, frugal meal. You can top it with additional cheese, too.

Thrifty and delicious summer salads

There are all sorts of reasons that cold salads have been a summer fixture for many decades, not the least of which is the fact that they're a very frugal side dish.

I keep these salads in the fridge all summer to add to a meal that has been cooked outside.

Granny's slaw

This is a coleslaw that my Granny used to make for my father, who was allergic to eggs. I've also adapted this to a home-canned version so we can enjoy it year-round.

Dressing:

- 3 tbsp of sugar
- 1 tsp of dry mustard powder
- 1/2 tsp of whole celery seeds
- 2 tbsp of cooking oil (sunflower is a nice light choice)
- 1/4 cup of white vinegar

Slaw:

- Half a head of cabbage, shredded, or a couple of those little pre-cut bags at the store (purple cabbage makes a beautiful dish)
- 1 large carrot, peeled
- 1 small white onion
- 1/2 bell pepper, any color

Directions:

1. Mix the dressing ingredients in a large bowl.
2. Use a food processor to chop the slaw ingredients. Be sure not to puree them – you just want a grated consistency.
3. Stir the veggies into the dressing and combine it well.
4. Cover the mixture with plastic wrap and let it sit in the fridge for at least an hour before serving. (Overnight is even better.)

Martha-ish potato salad

This potato salad recipe is adapted from an old Martha Stewart recipe. (When I first got married, my mother-in-law got me a subscription to Martha Stewart Living magazine. I learned to cook using her Cooking 101 recipes, and they are still the ones I swear by.)

The trick is to put the vinegar on your potatoes while they're still hot, so they absorb the tangy flavor.

Ingredients:

- 3 pounds of cubed potatoes
- 3 green onions, finely chopped
- 1/3 cup of white vinegar
- 3 boiled eggs, chopped
- ½-1 cup of mayo, depending how creamy you like it
- 1 tsp of dill weed
- 1 tsp of dry mustard
- Salt and pepper to taste

Directions:

1. Boil potatoes until they are firm yet tender, about 15 minutes.
2. Drain the potatoes, then immediately sprinkle them with vinegar and toss them.
3. Allow the potatoes to cool with the vinegar on them.
4. Mix the seasonings with the mayo, then stir in the potatoes and egg.
5. Refrigerate for at least an hour before serving.

Ranch potato salad

When my daughter was little, she was allergic to eggs. I adapted a potato salad that she could eat using this one brand of bottled ranch dressing which didn't contain egg. (Sadly, it's no longer available.)

Ingredients:

- 3 pounds of potatoes, diced
- ½ cup of your favorite Ranch salad dressing
- ½ cup of sour cream
- 2 tbsp of freeze-dried chives
- ¼ cup of shredded cheddar cheese
- Optional: 3 slices of bacon, cooked until crisp

Directions:

1. Boil potatoes until they are firm yet tender, about 15 minutes.
2. Drain the potatoes, then let them cool completely.
3. In a large bowl, mix the ranch and sour cream.
4. Stir in the cooled potatoes and dried chives.
5. Top with cheddar cheese and crumbled bacon.
6. Refrigerate for at least an hour before serving, then stir in the cheese and bacon.

Macaroni salad

This is an adaptation to a macaroni salad recipe that I got on the back of a box of mayonnaise years ago. I replaced celery with cucumber and made some other minor changes.

Ingredients:

- 2 cups of dry macaroni
- 1 cup of mayonnaise
- 2 tbsp of white vinegar
- 1 tbsp of prepared mustard
- 1 tsp of white sugar
- 1 cup of diced cucumber (or thinly sliced celery)
- 1 cup chopped green or red bell pepper
- 1/4 cup chopped onion
- Salt and pepper to taste

Directions:

1. Cook the macaroni until it's al dente.
2. Drain and rinse it with cold water until completely cool.
3. Combine mayo, vinegar, mustard, sugar, salt, and pepper in a large bowl.

4. Stir in macaroni, cucumber, bell pepper, and onion.
5. Refrigerate for an hour before serving.

Summer salads are the best

I love these side dishes because you can keep them in the fridge for several days. With the addition of a can of tuna, some of them can become lunch, or you can leave them as-is for a tasty side without heating up the kitchen.

Thrifty summer meals you can cook outside

If you are lucky enough to have a fire pit in your backyard, thrifty summer meals are yours, and you won't even have to heat up your house. No firepit? No problem! There's a section below on tinfoil packet meals you can cook on any type of outdoor grill.

Food on a stick

My kids have always delighted in cooking "food on a stick." There's something about roasting your own meal over the flames that most kids enjoy. Here are some of our best ideas. And no, I promise, we don't eat hot dogs all the time – just once in a while during the summer. The type of hot dog you get will give you some flexibility with regard to whether it's reasonably healthy or not.

- **Marshmallows:** Duh – that's kind of a classic, isn't it? You can take it a step further and turn your roasted marshmallow into a S'more by popping it on a square of chocolate between two graham crackers.
- **Octodogs:** I'm not much of a hot dog fan but once in a while we'll have them cooked on a campfire. If you cut them into "octodogs" you'll get the tasty crispness on more of the surface of the hot dog. Simply slice the hot dog at one end, longways, to make "legs." Then put your roasting fork into the uncut end of the hotdog and cook it over the flames until you've reached the desired degree of doneness. The "legs" will curl up, making it into an "octodog."
- **Pigs in a sleeping bag:** Usually they'd be pigs in a blanket, but this is a campfire! Place your hot dog longways on your skewer. Then, use crescent roll dough to wrap around the hot dog. Wrap this very loosely in foil and let the kids roast away above the flames. It will take about 15-20 minutes for the dough to get cooked and for the hot dog to get crispy.
- **Campfire crescent rolls:** Use your crescent roll

dough to wrap around your roasting stick. Use the coals and not the flames for cooking this. Rotate your stick slowly over the coals so that your bread rises and gets brown. It takes 5-10 minutes to get your crescents done. When you're ready to eat them, simply tear strips off your stick and enjoy with the rest of your meal.

- **Cinnamon Roll Skewers:** If you want some dessert, you can make that on a stick too. Using the ever-so-popular crescent roll dough, wind it around your skewer as above. But this time, before you cook it, roll it in a cinnamon sugar mixture to coat it with tasty goodness. Then, cook it over the coals for about 5-ish minutes until the dough is no longer gooey and the outside is crisp and lightly browned.

Campfire pizza

Don't forget campfire pizza! You'll need a Dutch oven for this one.

Ingredients

- Premade pizza crust*
- Marinara sauce of your choice
- 2 cups of shredded cheese

- Your favorite pizza toppings

Directions:

1. Grease the Dutch oven well and then place the crust on the bottom of it.
2. Top the crust with sauce, half the cheese, pizza toppings, and the other half of the cheese.
3. Put on the lid and place the Dutch oven on the coals. Add a few coals to the top of it and leave it alone for about 10 minutes.
4. Let it cool for 5 minutes, then slice it into triangles and scoop it out to serve it.

*If you want to use homemade pizza dough, pop it into the greased Dutch oven and cook it for 5 minutes in the coals before adding your sauce, cheese, and toppings. Then carry on with the rest of the instructions.

Tinfoil packet meals on the grill

One of the easiest ways to cook outside is by wrapping your meal in a packet of tinfoil. You can use any type of grill for the following meals. Another bonus is that you can customize the meals for family members with allergies or picky tendencies.

- **Sausage and peppers:** Place bell pepper and onion slices on the bottom of your foil and top it with your favorite sausage. (We enjoy bratwurst for this.) You can add some minced garlic or even a whole clove of it. Wrap it up tightly and pop it on the grill for about 20 minutes.
- **Garlic potatoes with cheese:** Cut up your potatoes into thin wedges. In a bowl, mix olive oil, minced garlic, garlic powder, onion powder, salt, pepper, and optional finely minced onion. Stir the potato wedges into the oil mixture, then place single servings of potatoes onto pieces of foil. Spoon any left-over olive oil mixture over the potatoes, then seal up the foil packets. Grill for 30 minutes, then open the packets and sprinkle on shredded cheddar cheese. Allow the cheese to melt, and then serve with sour cream.
- **Mexican chicken packets:** Mix corn, black beans, salsa, and chili powder, then drain off the liquid. Place one serving of the mixture on a piece of foil. Top this with a skinless, boneless chicken breast. Sprinkle cumin, salt, pepper, chili powder, and lime juice on top of the chicken. Seal the packet and grill for 30-45 minutes or until the chicken is done. Flip the packets every 15 minutes.

- **Pork Chops and Veggies:** Put some olive oil on each piece of tin foil. Add a mixture of your favorite veggies. We like green beans (they can be fresh or frozen), bell peppers, and onions. Feel free to use your family's favorite vegetables. Top this with a pork chop, then season this with soy sauce and some bottled plum or duck sauce from the Chinese section of your grocery store. Grill for 30-45 minutes or until the pork is done, flipping the packets every 15 minutes.
- **BBQ Cheesesteak Sandwich:** Cut a loaf of good quality bread longways. Add a little bit of olive oil to a piece of aluminum foil big enough to wrap around the entire sandwich. Place the bottom piece of bread on the foil, spread it with garlic butter, then top it with thin-sliced roast beef, a mixture of bell pepper and onion slices, and mushroom all very thinly sliced. Pop some mozzarella cheese slices on top of that, then add the top layer of bread. (Be sure to add garlic butter to that bread, too. Wrap the whole thing up in foil and put it on the grill for 30 minutes, flipping once.
- **Grilled quesadillas:** For each quesadilla, place a tortilla on a piece of foil. Tip it with refried beans, whatever meat you have cooked already, a dash of salsa, and some shredded cheese. Fold the tortilla over to make a half-moon shape, and then cover it with foil, leaving the ends of your packet open. Grill

it for 15 minutes, then check to see if the cheese is melted and the tortilla is crisp. If not, use tongs to flip the packet and let it cook for another ten minutes. Let it cool a bit, then slice and enjoy.

- **Side dish veggies:** This is so simple it's almost embarrassing. But...when you're grilling up some protein, you can make this simple, tasty side dish for the whole family at the cost of about $1. Grab a bag of mixed veggies from the grocery store freezer aisle. Plop a little pat of butter on each piece of tin foil then divvy up your bag of veggies. Sprinkle your favorite seasonings on top (we like MSG-free seasoning salt) or leave them simple. Add a little more butter if desired, then wrap your foil pouch tightly. It will take about 20-30 minutes for your vegetables to be fully cooked. Be sure to flip the packet every 10 minutes so the contents don't burn.

With these general ideas, feel free to experiment with what you have on hand! You have an idea of how long things need to cook and the formats you can use, so the sky is the limit for making creative, individual meals for your family members.

Keep your cool with thrifty summer meals

Your family will love the smoky taste of the foil packet food and food on a stick, and you'll saving money by using these simple, inexpensive ingredients and NOT making your air-conditioner combat the heat of cooking indoors. Plus, what's more fun than a campfire or barbecue?

Autumn

There are many delicious things in season during the fall. If you live in a warmer climate, summer produce may continue to be available through the end of September.

- Apples
- Beets
- Broccoli
- Brussel Sprouts
- Cabbage
- Carrots
- Cauliflower
- Celery Root
- Cranberries
- Dates
- Fennel
- Garlic

- Ginger
- Grapes
- Green Beans
- Iceberg Lettuce
- Leaf Lettuce
- Mushrooms
- Nuts
- Okra
- Parsnips
- Pears
- Pumpkins
- Sweet Potatoes and Yams
- Winter Squash

Fall food is all about the cozy, carby goodness.

Fruit salsa with cinnamon chips

Ingredients for salsa

- 4 red apples
- 4 green pears
- 2 tbsp of lemon juice
- 3 tbsp of brown sugar
- 1 tbsp of cinnamon powder
- Chopped walnuts (optional)

Directions for salsa

1. Wash your fruit well, and leaving on the peel, dice it into uniform, bite-sized pieces.
2. Place the fruit in a large bowl and pour the lemon juice on top. Stir the fruit to mix the lemon juice through it.
3. Add the brown sugar to the top, then sprinkle on the cinnamon (spread it out so you don't get one bite that is super-cinnamon-y). Use two large spoons to toss the mixture and season the fruit.
4. If you're adding walnuts, sprinkle them on top. Refrigerate for at least an hour before serving.

Ingredients for Cinnamon Chips

- 8 soft flour tortillas
- 2 tbsp of melted butter or coconut oil
- A dish with 1-part cinnamon to 3 parts brown sugar – measurements are to taste

Directions for cinnamon chips

1. Preheat the oven to 350F.
2. Brush each tortilla with melted butter or coconut oil.

3. Sprinkle with the cinnamon-sugar mixture, then cut each tortilla into 8ths.
4. Put the triangles on a greased cookie sheet and bake for 8-10 minutes. You'll want to watch these closely. They should be light golden, but not too dark.

Serve cinnamon chips with fruit salsa. We used to take this dish to family get-togethers, and it was gone almost immediately!

Hey there, pumpkin

If you like to carve your Jack'O'Lantern just before Halloween so you can enjoy that pumpkin-y goodness, do I have some ideas for you! Check out these tasty pumpkin recipes to put them front and center on your table. Think of it as the Whole Buffalo Theory of Jack O'Lanterns.

All of these recipes use pumpkin that you have pre-cooked and mashed or pureed. (You can substitute one 15-ounce can of pumpkin for 2 cups of fresh pumpkin.)

Pumpkin Parmesan soup

Ingredients

- 2 cups of cooked pumpkin
- 1 medium onion
- 3 cloves of garlic
- 1 tbsp butter
- 1/4 cup of white wine (you can sub vegetable or chicken broth)
- 1/2 cup of milk (any kind)
- Parmesan cheese to taste
- Optional garnishes: Sage, basil, pumpkin seeds

Directions

1. Finely chop onion and garlic.
2. Heat the butter in a saucepan and saute your onion and garlic until fragrant.
3. Turn down the heat and add a splash of dry white wine
4. Add in 2 cups of pumpkin and 1//2 cup of milk. Let it simmer for 5 minutes.
5. Finely dice sage and/or basil and stir it in.
6. Add Parmesan cheese to taste and continue to heat it up until the cheese is melted.

Serve this with some crusty sourdough bread.

Pumpkin gnocchi

Ingredients

- 2 cups of cooked pumpkin
- 1 ½ cup flour
- Salt and pepper to taste

Directions

1. Combine all the ingredients and knead well. You want a sticky and fluffy dough.
2. Roll the dough into a log and cut it into quarters.
3. Roll the quarters into smaller logs,
4. Slice the logs into ½ inch pieces, press with a fork, and put them into a pot of salted boiling water until they float.

For an extra delicious texture, fry the cooked gnocchi with butter and sage. We like to serve this with poultry.

Pumpkin pasta sauce

Ingredients

- 2 cups of cooked pumpkin
- 1 tbsp of butter
- 3 cloves of garlic
- 1/4 cup of white wine or veggie broth
- Salt, pepper, and crushed red chilis to taste
- 1-4 tbsp Parmesan cheese

Directions

1. Heat up the butter, then add your garlic and saute it until it's fragrant.
2. Stir in the rest of the ingredients and allow it to simmer with the lid off for 5 minutes.
3. Stir in some Parmesan cheese to taste to help thicken it up.

Toss the sauce with your favorite pasta and serve it with bread and salad.

Pumpkin pie dip

This is the only dessert-y one in the mix, but I love how lazy it is. My kids enjoyed it far more than pumpkin pie.

Ingredients

- 2 cups of cooked pumpkin puree
- 1 container of whipped cream cheese
- ½ cup brown sugar
- Pumpkin pie spice to taste

Directions

1. Pop all the ingredients into a food processor or use a mixer to combine them well.
2. Let the mixture sit in the fridge until serving time.

Serve with graham crackers or nilla wafers for dipping.

Jamaican pumpkin soup

Ingredients:

- 4 cups of pumpkin, peeled and cut into chunks
- 2 tbsp coconut oil or butter
- 1 cup of minced onion
- 3 cloves garlic, minced
- 1/4 cup of chopped celery1 cup of diced carrot
- 1 cup of diced potato
- 1 tsp of dried parsley
- 1/4 tsp of dried thyme
- 1/4 tsp of cayenne pepper
- 1/4 tsp of ground allspice
- 4 cups of water (you can also use chicken or veggie broth)
- Salt and pepper to taste
- Garnish: Unsweetened coconut milk or sour cream, chopped green onions

Directions:

- Heat the oil or butter in a stockpot and sauté the onion and garlic until it is golden and fragrant. Add in the celery and carrot and continue to cook for 3 more minutes.

- Add in all the rest of the ingredients except the garnish.
- Bring this to a boil, then reduce it to a simmer for half an hour to 45 minutes.
- Use a stick blender or food processor to puree the soup.
- Serve immediately with a garnish of coconut milk or sour cream and chopped green onions.

Variation: If you want to cook up some boneless chicken thighs and season them with the spices in the recipe, they can be chopped and added to the soup after pureeing for a heartier meal.

Carrot fries

I often serve this side dish as a nutritious replacement for French fries.

Ingredients:

- 4 cups of carrots, sliced into coins or sticks
- 3 tbsp. of olive oil
- 1 tsp of garlic powder
- 1 tsp of onion powder

- 1 tsp of seasoning salt (no msg)
- 1/2 tsp of cayenne pepper (optional)

Directions:

- Preheat the oven to 425F.
- In a large bowl, mix seasonings into olive oil.
- Stir in carrot slices and toss until they are well coated.
- Spread the carrots on a cookie sheet in a single layer.
- Bake for 20 minutes, then flip the carrots to get them evenly browned.
- Return to the oven for another 10-15 minutes until the carrots are crisp and lightly golden.

Serve with yogurt ranch dip or barbecue sauce.

Winter

Just because it's winter, that doesn't mean there's nothing in season. Now is the time to tuck into those hearty root vegetables. You can also get some lovely citrus.

- Beets
- Broccoli

- Brussel Sprouts
- Cabbage
- Carrots
- Cauliflower
- Celeriac
- Grapefruit
- Kale
- Leeks
- Lemons
- Mushrooms
- Onions
- Oranges
- Parsnip
- Potatoes
- Rutabagas
- Sweet Potatoes and Yams
- Turnips
- Winter Squash

Here are just a few ways to add a little more cabbage to your life

Try these tips from my eldest daughter.

- Add it to your soup or stew
- Shred it and add it to casseroles

- Make coleslaw with it
- Add it to a stir-fry
- Cabbage rolls
- Fry it up with some onion
- Steam it
- Roast it (This one is super easy – cut it in thick chunks, brush it with a little oil, maybe throw in some garlic, and roast at 350 F for about 25 minutes.)
- Fry it with your morning eggs
- Added to your dish of pierogies and topped with sour cream and cheese
- Corned beef and cabbage – a staple of Irish cuisine.

How do you prepare winter vegetables?

If you hand some folks a rutabaga, they'll have no idea what to do with it. Probably one of the most common reasons that people pass on the winter vegetables is because they don't know how to prepare them. Invest in some great cookbooks for inspiration. I like Depression-era cookbooks for simple instructions on preparation, and there are some wonderful locavore cookbooks on the market that will teach you to turn these humble-looking veggies into mouth-watering treats.

Switch your salads to ones like coleslaw or broccoli salad, and switch out your warm-weather greens for kale. Kale usually needs the addition of some sweetness – try adding honey to your salad dressing or tossing in a handful of dried cranberries.

Roasting your veggies brings out the sweet flavor while also warming up the house. Brussels sprouts, cauliflower, broccoli, and carrots can be roasted with garlic and olive oil for a nutritious side. My family also loves "oven fries" made from root vegetables.

Potatoes are always a welcome dish, whether they're mashed, roasted, fried, or baked.

Winter vegetable substitutions

You can also make your regular dishes but substitute in some winter produce.

- **Potato**: Try sweet potato, parsnip, rutabaga, cauliflower, turnips, celeriac, or squash
- **Summer squash**: Try winter squash or rutabaga
- **Romaine lettuce or baby spinach**: Try kale or shredded cabbage
- **Asparagus**: Try broccoli or Brussels sprouts
- **Carrots**: Try parsnips or turnip slices

How do you cut up root vegetables?

You have a lumpy pile of unfamiliar produce on your cutting board. What the heck do you do with *that*?

Part of the reason people are hesitant to try new vegetables is that they honestly have no idea how to cook them. They're rustic-looking, unfamiliar, and intimidating to some.

Celeriac, rutabaga, turnips, and parsnips – all these are root vegetables and can be treated just like a potato. You can mash them, slice them and fry them, add them to stew in chunks, puree them into a soup, or roast them.

Anytime you have a vegetable that is unfamiliar, the simplest way to deal with it is to slice off the ends so you can see what you have to work with. Then once you've seen the thickness of the skin, you can peel them using the most applicable method.

A turnip has the thinnest skin. You could use a vegetable peeler for that. The skin of the rutabaga and celeriac will require a sturdy paring knife. At this point, you can cut your unfamiliar vegetable in half to discern whether or not there's a core to deal with. These particular vegetables can be treated the same way you would a potato – there isn't a core of any type inside.

Random roasted winter vegetables with herbs

This recipe is very flexible – you're just going to use what you have on hand. Therefore, I did not include a lot of measurements – eyeball it like the bad-to-the-bone frugal cook that you are. ●

Ingredients:

- 3-5 cups of chopped, peeled root vegetables, any proportion: turnips, carrots, potatoes, parsnips, celeriac, rutabagas, beets, onion – whatever you have available
- 2-3 tbsp of olive oil
- Minced garlic to taste
- Seasonings of choice: minced garlic, chopped onion, salt, fresh cracked pepper, parsley, thyme, Hungarian paprika, and celery seed. If you have fresh herbs, throw those in, too. You can also use a general seasoning salt or a mixture like Mrs. Dash
- 2-3 pieces of bacon (optional)

Directions:

- Preheat your oven to 400F.
- Once they're peeled and cut into chunks, put the vegetables in a large bowl and use a rubber spatula to toss them with some olive oil and the seasoning of your choice.
- Spread them on a large cookie sheet.
- You can add a few slices of bacon to the top of our mixture if you eat meat, but that's entirely optional.
- Slide the tray of veggies onto the top rack of the oven and set the timer for 50 minutes.
- You'll want to stir the veggies once or twice during the roasting time to ensure they don't stick and that they get deliciously golden brown on all sides.
- When they're done, they should be fork-tender, but lightly crisp on the outside.

If you have leftovers (we never do!), you can puree them and add them to potato soup for a hearty winter meal. Alternatively, pop them back in a 400F oven to reheat them and keep the glorious texture.

Lazy ala Daisy

I spent a decade as a working single mama. Ten hours a day outside the home, then dashing around to after-school activities, errands, and whatever else had to be jammed in, all the while trying to make ends meet and keep us fed. Because of that, I learned the difficult lesson that time is money.

While I would have loved to make every single bite my children ate from scratch using strictly organic ingredients that I carefully sourced locally, the only way I could have done that is if I didn't sleep a wink. So...I developed some shortcuts.

Many of these shortcuts are not as cheap as making the same thing from scratch, but the ability to put together a meal my kids clamored to eat in minutes, instead of hitting up the drive-through on the way home from work, was in itself a saving. Here are a few ways to get your meals on the table faster.

Frugal Food Prep Keeps You On-Budget

Back when I worked outside the home, Sunday afternoon was always dedicated to weekly food prep. It was absolutely necessary to be able to juggle all of my responsibilities during the week ahead. Now that I work from home, I usually break food prep into two sessions, but the basic premise is the same.

There are a lot of time-saving benefits to this.

You only have one big kitchen clean-up. The rest of the week your dishes only consist of your plates and flatware, and what you used to heat your food in.

You can multitask by having several things in the oven cooking at once – this also saves on your utility bill. You can also wash and prep all your produce at the same time, and then just wash your colander and cutting board when you're finished.

Throughout the week meals are strictly grab-and-go. If your food is already prepped, dinner can be on the table in 10-15 minutes every night.

What does a food prep afternoon typically consist of?

I like to get everything done during one busy day. We have generally used Sunday afternoon for our food-prep day. On Sunday, I do the following tasks.

- Menu planning
- Grocery shopping
- Washing and cutting up vegetables
- Washing fruit
- Portioning out snacks for lunch boxes
- Doing the baking
- Preparing some basic items that can be used in different ways throughout the week (chicken, beef, grains, salad)

As soon as we return from the grocery store, we begin prepping food before it gets put away. I fire up the oven to preheat it, get the oven foods ready to go bake, and then slice up and portion out the vegetables for the refrigerator.

There are so many benefits to this.

When you prepare your food ahead of time, dinner is on the table faster than you can say "drive-thru". Your budget will thank you because you won't require those impromptu pizza deliveries when you just don't feel like cooking. Your waistline will thank you because you won't grab high-calorie, low-nutrient convenience foods. Your health will thank you because you will be eating nutritious, wholesome foods from scratch that nourish you.

And don't look at it as another miserable chore to add to your weekly tasks. Pick an afternoon you have free, turn on the tunes, don a kitschy crazy apron, and start cooking. It's even more fun if you get the whole family involved.

Here's a sample menu.

Here's a sample list of foods that we made one weekend during our food prep frenzy.

- Meatloaf "muffins"
- Baked brown rice
- A whole chicken
- Veggies for steaming
- Roasted Brussels sprouts
- Blueberry corn muffins (for breakfast)
- Boiled eggs (for breakfasts and lunches)
- Wheatberry Pilaf
- Broccoli slaw with bacon

- Veggies packets for lunchboxes
- Bread

We have a big dinner on Sunday night with plenty of leftovers. Food is packaged for the week, with lunches being packed into divided containers, and the rest of the food being refrigerated in larger containers.

Other things that work well for food prep:

- Dips (hummus or sour cream-based)
- Soup
- Chili
- Meatballs
- Taco fillings
- Salad
- Grilled meat
- Roasted vegetables
- Falafel
- Beans
- Baked goods

I only store the prepped food in the refrigerator through Thursday at the very latest. If you need to keep your food longer than that, you should store it in the freezer for food safety purposes.

What does the menu look like?

Wondering what meals we make with all that? I'm not an especially "fancy" cook, so you'll find that these are simple, balanced meals the whole family will enjoy.

For dinner on a week like the one above:

- **Sunday**: Roasted chicken, roasted brussels sprouts, wheatberry pilaf, and homemade bread
- **Monday**: Meatloaf muffins, mashed rutabaga, and steamed veggies
- **Tuesday**: Leftover chicken stirfried with prepped veggies and rice (Any remaining chicken goes in the freezer)
- **Wednesday**: Meatloaf with gravy on homemade rolls, sauteed mushrooms, broccoli slaw, leftover rutabaga
- **Thursday**: A whatever is left free-for-all, fondly known as "Leftover Buffet"
- **Friday**: Homemade pizza topped with chicken, veggies, and barbecue sauce
- **Saturday**: Breakfast for dinner with eggs, toasted homemade bread, bacon or sausage, and fruit

As mentioned above, we eat muffins with fruit for breakfast throughout the week, and we use leftovers as lunches. As you practice with your favorite recipes, you'll discover some things reheat far better than others. Take note of the things your family enjoys most.

If you don't like to prep everything ahead of time, read on for more timesavers!

Tasty Ways to Save Time with Breaded Chicken

Whether you make them yourself on food prep day or get a great deal on ready-made ones for the freezer, breaded boneless chicken cutlets or strips are incredibly versatile meal starters that can save you both time and money. And let's face it, sometimes saving time allows us to save money because it prevents an order to Doordash or a trip through the drive-through.

I'm just trying to be real here – we don't always want (or have time) to make every single meal from scratch every single time we eat. If you'd never ever ever use any of these shortcuts, that's awesome! This roundup is here for the folks who do, from time to time, turn to some prepped ingredients for meals.

Here are some delicious ways to use them with simple sauces you can create on a dime. These are all tested and true with my family, and big hits. They taste a lot like restaurant meals but at a fraction of the price.

Boneless "wings"

Want the flavor of boneless chicken wings without the work or the high price? Use pre-breaded chicken strips to make your own.

1. Simply prepare the strips in your oven or air fryer as per directions.
2. In a large bowl, mix up your favorite wing sauce. We like to mix a sweet barbecue sauce with some Frank's red hot or a similar hot sauce.
3. Toss the hot strips generously in the sauce.

Serve this with carrot sticks, celery, and either ranch or bleu cheese dressing.

Hot honey chicken sandwiches

Hot honey chicken is all the rage and this easy hack will have it on the table faster than you can hit a drive-thru.

1. Prepare your chicken in an air fryer or oven as per

directions.

2. In a saucepan, combine honey, hot sauce (something along the lines of Franks), cayenne pepper, chili powder, onion powder, garlic powder, black pepper, and a smidge of salt.
3. Drizzle the honey sauce over the hot, crisp chicken.
4. Plop it on a toasted hamburger bun with some ranch dressing and shredded lettuce. Serve immediately with fries. (I usually cook oven fries while I'm cooking the chicken.)

Lazy chicken parm

I love love love chicken parmesan, and obviously, as a bit of an Italian food purist, I'd rather eat the kind that a grandma slaves over lovingly for hours. BUT – with no such Nonna in sight, sometimes you have to hack it.

1. Prepare your chicken in an air fryer or oven as per directions. Use a pan with sides so you can add the sauce directly to it when the time comes.
2. Pop open a jar of marinara sauce (either homemade or good storebought) and dump the entire thing in the pan with the chicken.
3. Top this with some parmesan cheese and mozzarella, then pop it back in the oven and bake it

until the sauce is heated through and the cheese is fabulously gooey.

Serve it with spaghetti tossed with olive oil and garlic, some crispy bread, and a salad if you're really getting fancy. You can also serve it on toasted baguettes for a chicken parm grinder, ala NYC.

Orange chicken

If you love Panda Express orange chicken as much as my family does, you'll probably like this little copycat. This works better with chicken strips or nuggets.

1. Prepare your chicken in an air fryer or oven as per directions.
2. In a saucepan, combine 2/3 cup of orange marmalade, 3 tbsp soy sauce, a splash of vinegar, some powdered ginger, some garlic powder, and crushed chili peppers if you like it spicy.
3. Heat it up until you can combine it thoroughly.
4. Toss your prepared chicken in the sauce.

Serve this over a bowl of rice and steamed veggies. (Broccoli and green beans are very tasty with this.)

Chicken and waffles

I'll be honest – I'm totally NOT a chicken and waffle fans. But one of my daughters just loves it and you can easily hack it with some freezer items.

1. Prepare your chicken in an air fryer or oven as per directions.
2. Mix your maple syrup with a sprinkling of cayenne pepper for kick and butter for saltiness.
3. Make waffles (either the toaster kind of from scratch.)

Assemble this by plopping your prepared chicken onto your prepared waffles and drenching the whole thing with your sweet-spicy-salty syrup. Voila!

Chicken fried chicken

This Southern delight relies on the white gravy for the wow factor.

1. Prepare your chicken in an air fryer or oven as per directions.
2. Meanwhile, make a batch of white gravy. Heat up 2 tbsp of meat drippings, then whisk in 3 tbsp of flour

and 2 cups of milk. Add salt and pepper to taste

3. Drench your prepared chicken with white gravy then add a whole lot more black pepper than you think you need.

Serve this with mashed potatoes and a veggie for a hearty Southern-style meal.

"Fried" chicken salad

1. Prepare your chicken in an air fryer or oven as per directions.
2. Put the chicken aside and let it cool.
3. Meanwhile, assemble your salad. I like to use greens like romaine or baby spinach, carrots, tomatoes, cucumbers, and some corn.
4. Slice up the chicken on top of the salad.

Douse it in ranch dressing, toss, and serve.

Lazy Daisy Cordon Bleu stacks

Some of us are kind of lazy. There, I said it. I love Cordon Bleu chicken, but i don't love the work involved in pounding the chicken and rolling it up. So, I do a lazy version.

1. Prepare your chicken in an air fryer or oven as per directions, pulling it out of the oven 5 minutes before it's done.
2. Top it with thin-sliced ham and swiss cheese.
3. Put it back in the oven and make the sauce. Melt 2 tbsp of butter then whisk in 2 tbsp of flour. Slowly whisk in one cup of milk, then 1 tbsp of dijon mustard. Add a splash of Worcestershire sauce and then up to 1/2 a cup of Parmesan cheese. Stir frequently as the sauce thickens.
4. Once the sauce is ready, pop the chicken, ham, and cheese stacks on a plate and cover them with sauce.

Serve this with buttered rice and steamed veggies. (Asparagus is especially tasty.)

Chicken ranch wraps

Here's an easy-peasy meal for any cold-breaded chicken you happen to have in the fridge.

1. Slice your breaded chicken into bite-sized pieces.
2. I like to toss the filling like a salad instead of

slathering ranch on the tortilla. In a bowl, toss together chicken, shredded lettuce, ripe tomatoes, crisp bacon, and some shredded cheese. You can also add some avocado or other produce if you wish.

3. Put it in the center of the wrap. Fold over the end, then roll the wrap up tightly.

Serve it with a handful of chips or some veggie sticks.

Fake Fil-A Sandwiches

If you are a Chik Fil-A fan, here's a knockoff sandwich you might enjoy.

1. Prepare your chicken in an air fryer or oven as per directions.
2. Put mayo on a bun. I like a metric crap-ton of mayo but use your desired amount.
3. Plop on some lettuce and some good dill pickles, then top it with your cooked chicken.

If you want to be authentic, serve it with waffle fries. However, if you don't care too much about authenticity, any fries will do.

Thrifty Homemade Pizza Using Premade Crusts

Your premade crust can be premade by you or premade by the store. Here are some options.

The Crust of Your Homemade Pizza

The best supporting actor in the cast of pizza is, of course, the crust. There are all sorts of bases for a pizza, but here are some of the ones we find to be the tastiest and thriftiest. These doughs work for all of the recipes except the deep dish one, in which the crust is the star of the show.

Don't be overwhelmed by making scratch pizza dough. Most of the time to make it is hands-off.

From Scratch

Here's my favorite simple pizza dough recipe.

Ingredients

- 3 to 3.5 cups of flour
- 1 cup of warm water
- 1 tbsp of sugar
- 2 1/4 tsp of active dry yeast
- 3 tbsp of olive oil
- 1 tsp salt

Directions

1. Stir water, sugar, and yeast together and allow it to sit for 5 minutes.
2. Add olive oil and salt, then stir in the flour until well blended.
3. Knead the dough for about 5 minutes, then let it rise, covered, for 30 minutes.
4. Preheat the oven to 425F.
5. Knead the dough again, then roll it out.
6. Top it with your desired toppings.
7. Bake for 15-20 minutes, or until lightly golden brown.

If you get your yeast in bulk is way more thrifty than in those little packets. You can use this for regular pizza or pockets/calzones.

Sort of Scratch

Next, we have "sort of scratch." These doughs take a wee bit of work but not quite as much as making it from scratch. But keep in mind, we pay for the time of others. These shortcuts add money to the price of your pizza.

- Refrigerated dough (none of the mixing, only some rising and rolling)
- Crescent roll dough pizza (get off-brand)
- Bisquik pizza (find recipes online)

Convenient

If you're in a hurry, there are ways to get around making your own dough.

- Pizza crusts (the ones in the bread aisle are less expensive than the ones in the freezer aisle)
- Pitas (the nice thick ones)
- Tortillas (for thin crust personal pizzas – this was a family favorite for my kiddos, and it's very inexpensive)

Now that you've got your base all set, it's time to top some pizzas!

Classic Homemade Pizza

Pizza is a classic for a reason. Ordinary, everyday pizza is a hit for just about everyone.

Sauce:

- Canned spaghetti sauce
- Jarred spaghetti sauce
- Small can of pizza sauce
- Crushed tomatoes seasoned with basil, garlic powder, onion powder, oregano, and thyme
- Homemade marinara sauce

Toppings:

We all have our favorite pizza toppings, so use those here. I like to keep pepperoni, a bag of sauteed peppers and onions, and diced ham in the freezer to top an emergency pizza fast. But think about your family's last pizza order – keep that stuff on hand for the most authentic take-out-fake-out possible.

Cheese:

Use your favorite cheese to top your pizza. We like a blend of mozzarella and parmesan. If you shred it yourself, you save much0-moolah over the bags of pre-shredded cheese.

Mexican Pizza

This was a household staple when my kiddos were growing up. It's filling, frugal, and delicious.

Ingredients:

- Refried beans (canned or homemade)
- Salsa (from the store or homemade)
- Ground beef (or ground whatever-floats-your-boat)
- Taco seasoning
- Diced veggies: tomato, peppers, onions
- Cheese (cheddar is a great option)

Directions:

1. Cook your ground beef in a skillet with taco

seasoning. About 1/4 pound of beef is plenty for one pizza, but add more if you want it meatier.

2. Spread refried beans on the pizza crust of your choice.
3. Spoon some salsa on top of it.
4. Top it with cheese, then veggies.
5. Sprinkle a tiny bit more taco seasoning on top.
6. Bake it according to the needs of your crust or until everything is melty and hot.

Allow it to cool for 10 minutes before slicing. You may want to serve this with sour cream or more salsa for dipping.

White Pizza

The trick to white pizza is to pre-bake your dough before adding your toppings.

Toppings:

- Olive oil seasoned with either fresh garlic or garlic powder.
- Ricotta cheese (or whip up cottage cheese in the food processor for a cheaper version)

- Mozzarella (the tastiest is the balls of fresh mozzarella, thinly sliced; the easiest is pre-shredded mozzarella; the cheapest is to shred your own mozzarella from a brick of cheese)
- Parmesan
- Dried herbs: Italian seasoning blend, OR oregano, basil, parsley

Directions:

1. Brush the crust with seasoned olive oil.
2. Spread ricotta or whipped cottage cheese over it.
3. Top it with mozzarella and parmesan.
4. Sprinkle herbs on top.
5. Bake it at 425 for 10-15 minutes until gloriously gooey and melty.

You can also add very finely chopped spinach and grilled chicken to this pizza to make it a bit more filling.

No-Cheese Pizza

No cheese? Is she CRAZY?

Well, yes, but not because of the no-cheese pizza. In this pizza, the toppings are the stars of the show. In Italy, one version of this is called Pizza Marinara. I only make this with homemade pizza dough because I want everything present to be top quality.

- Pizza dough (homemade or store-bought dough)
- Marinara sauce (go with a really good one – I prefer homemade for this)

Topping Options:

- Fresh herbs (head out to your garden and get some oregano and basil)
- Meat (I like to make this with ground beef, sausage crumbles, pepperoni, and ham)
- Veggie (peppers, onions, mushrooms, tomatoes, herbs)

The key is LOTS of toppings. You won't miss the cheese if you use good ingredients.

Breakfast Pizza

Pizza for breakfast? Yes PLEASE.

I like to use a base that is more common to breakfast food, like the DIY Bisquik recipe above or crescent roll dough. (Get the off-brand.) You can also use English muffins and make personal pizzas.

I use the same kind of sauce I'd use for classic pizza when I make breakfast pizza, but some folks like it better "white pizza" style with just the addition of breakfast-y things.

Toppings:

- Scrambled eggs
- Whole eggs cracked on top, salted, and peppered
- Crumbled bacon
- Sausage
- Diced ham
- Onions
- Peppers
- Mushrooms
- Shredded cheese

Directions:

1. Preheat your oven to 400 degrees (or whatever your dough requires.) Pre-bake your dough if it isn't already cooked.
2. Add your toppings. If money is tight, you can use far less meat. Try chopping it up smaller to make it go further and lend its flavor.

3. If you're using raw eggs, make sure to cook them to your desired consistency. As a hater of runny eggs (don't hate me), I'd be devasted if I cut into my pizza and yellow goo ran all over it. But you might like that, so watch the eggs closely.
4. Bake this for approximately 10-12 minutes until your eggs are done and your cheese melts everything together into deliciousness.

Barbeque Chicken Pizza

This is so incredibly delicious and tastes positively gourmet. We always save our leftover chicken for this tasty purpose.

Toppings:

- Barbecue sauce of choice
- Cooked chicken off the bone
- Onions
- Hot Peppers
- Cheese

Directions:

1. Use the barbecue sauce like you would marinara and spread it all over your pizza crust.
2. Top it with chicken, diced onions and hot peppers, and cheese.
3. Bake it according to the needs of your crust.

Deep Dish Pizza

The star of deep dish pizza is, of course, the crust. That makes it filling and delicious. You can go all out and use a recipe for the dough, or you can take a shortcut and make your crust out of refrigerated biscuits – it depends on how much time you have.

I prefer to use my cast-iron skillet for deep-dish pizza. I always cook whatever meat I'm adding to the pizza in it to get a flavorful coating. Preheat your oven to 375.

You're going to FILL your pizza instead of topping your pizza.

I cook all my fillings and then mix in the sauce. Here are the things I use for deep-dish pizza:

- Sausage crumbles

- Ground beef
- Pepperoni (diced)
- Onions
- Mushrooms

Feel free to add all your favorites. Once the meat is cooked through, add the veggies and get them browned as well. Remove the toppings and put them into a large bowl. There, stir in your sauce.

Press the dough (whether biscuits or homemade) into your skillet **once it's cooled enough to touch**, and make it go all the way up the sides. Then brush the dough with butter seasoned with garlic powder.

Add half of your cheese of choice to the pizza dough in the skillet.

Pour in your fillings, and then top it with the rest of the cheese.

I like to put my skillet on a cookie sheet in case my pie runneth over. Bake it for 20-25 minutes. Check it halfway through – you may need to lay some foil over it to prevent the edges from getting overcooked.

Let your deep dish pizza sit for 10-15 minutes before slicing. This is an eat-with-a-knife-and-fork pizza, and it's super filling. One cast-iron skillet of pizza with a side of salad feeds all four of us, with nobody leaving hungry. This is so good that I often use it as a company meal.

The Budgetary Benefits of Breakfast for Dinner (and 50 Thrifty Ideas)

Looking for a way to save money on your grocery bill? Looking for a quick supper to feed your family when you're in a rush? Looking for something cozy and comforting to eat? Look no further than breakfast for dinner.

Breakfast is often the most frugal meal of the day for many of us. Think about common breakfast foods – yogurt and fruit, scrambled eggs and toast, oatmeal, pancakes....you see what I mean? None of these things cost a ton of money, but they're quick to put together (which means you won't be tempted to go out and grab a pizza), and they're satisfying.

Breakfasts are often heavy on grains and eggs, which, even in these days of inflation, are some of the thriftiest eats around. Really, the price of breakfast for dinner depends on you – your choices, your protein options, and the ratio of ingredients. It can be as cheap or as expensive as you want it to be. That's why the suggestions below, for the most part, are not recipes but ideas. You can make them fit your supplies and your budget.

Breakfast for dinner is cozy and satisfying.

A lot of folks, myself included, find breakfast to be the ultimate comfort food. I love sitting down to a big stack of pancakes with butter and maple syrup or a savory plate of eggs and potatoes. In a world where we're often in a rush, sometimes we only have breakfast food on the weekend, so that in itself makes breakfast for dinner feel like a decadent treat, even with humble ingredients.

If you spin it right, you can easily get your kids on board with this. I used to let my girls get into their PJs early and eat breakfast for dinner in front of the television. This gives breakfast for dinner a celebratory air while costing very little. As with any thrifty thing, it's all about the presentation.

Sometimes it's not about the presentation – it's just about quickly and inexpensively getting yourself fed after a long day. These are the moments you grab a bowl of cereal or you butter some toast and call it a day.

Whatever the reason, whatever the presentation method, breakfast for dinner offers a simple and inexpensive option for your menu.

50 Thrifty Breakfast for Dinner Ideas

Here are some tasty foods you can serve when you're having breakfast for dinner. Choose one or more of the following.

1. Scrambled eggs
2. Toast with butter
3. Biscuits and gravy
4. Fried potatoes
5. Cereal with milk
6. Oatmeal
7. Yogurt with fruit
8. Huevos rancheros (basically eggs with salsa and beans)
9. Pancakes
10. Omelets
11. Breakfast pizza
12. Waffles
13. Breakfast burritos
14. Grits
15. Rice porridge with brown sugar and cinnamon

16. Cornbread with butter and syrup
17. Breakfast sandwiches
18. Toast with peanut butter and jelly
19. Smoothies
20. Breakfast skillets with eggs, potatoes, and veggies
21. Chilaquiles and eggs
22. Frittatas
23. Breakfast bowls with fruit, a thick smoothie, and granola
24. English muffin with hummus
25. Egg in a hole
26. Bagel with cream cheese
27. Toast with banana and peanut butter
28. Cottage cheese and fruit
29. Homemade granola
30. Cream of wheat
31. Banana bread
32. Homemade hash skillet
33. Pancake and sausage roll-ups
34. Kolaches made with crescent roll dough
35. Savory crepes
36. French toast
37. Beans on toast
38. Breakfast cookies
39. Muffins and fruit
40. Apple sauce and graham crackers
41. Homemade granola bars and canned fruit
42. Zucchini bread

43. Potato pancakes
44. Breakfast stir fry (small amount of sausage, ham, or bacon, cooked with veggies and eggs, and served over rice)
45. Sheet pan eggs
46. Cinnamon rolls topped with crumbled bacon
47. Breakfast quesadillas
48. Greek yogurt with honey
49. Loaded breakfast potatoes
50. Shakshuka

Breakfast for dinner is always a winner!

Back in 2010, I hated my job. I hated my life. I was overspending and always broke, I worked constantly, and I was too exhausted to enjoy my time with my two daughters.

Like most stories of dramatic change, it starts out sad. But hang in there. It gets way better.

It took death to rock my world and inspire me to change everything. First, my beloved father died. I was devastated, but I made the funeral arrangements and helped my mother get her bearings. Then, I went back home with my kids, dreading my return to a job I was beginning to despise.

This happened as the automotive industry was collapsing. To keep myself employed, I was forced to survive on significantly lower pay for more work as others were let go. My financial situation began to unravel. I'd spent more money than I was making traveling back and forth from Canada to the southern US during my dad's terminal illness. But sometimes, you lose your handle on things like money during difficult times.

As a result, first, I lost my house. Then, I had to return my car because I couldn't make the payments. And then, just a few months later, everything got worse. My children's dad died. Suddenly. Shockingly. Gone at the age of 40.

In less than one year, the whole world was different. And we had to change with it.

In what probably sounds like the most ridiculous idea ever, I left my full-time job. Yeah. On purpose.

I accepted a severance package from the company (which was downsizing anyway), cashed in a small retirement fund, and set about to live a different life. I paid off my debts and started over. I wanted adventures and experiments and freedom. I wanted to live off-grid. I wanted to travel. I wanted to make a living writing. I didn't know how to do *any* of it. But I knew with every fiber of my being I was going to wholeheartedly embrace the chance to try.

So ever since, I've been doing cool and unusual things and prioritizing the way I spend my money to support the life

I always dreamed of living. I put two girls through college debt-free, I've lived in 5 different countries, I travel *a lot*, and I write full-time.

My life has been so incredible since I prioritized what I was willing to spend money on and took that first leap. I'm not wealthy, but I prioritize happiness. Sometimes I wake up in a new country with new morning sounds, and I smile because I can hardly believe that this is my life. I have absolutely everything I need and most of what I want. Can we really ask for more than that?

Check out my website, TheFrugalite.com, where I write about living a large life on a tiny budget. You'll find all sorts of money-saving mojo there.

I'm the founder of the popular website, TheOrganicPrepper.com, and the author of quite a few books on emergency preparedness, food, and frugality. You can find my books on Amazon, Barnes and Noble, and other popular booksellers. Check out *The Ultimate Guide to Frugal Living* for more great money-saving information like you read in this book.

Incidentally, thank you for buying it. I hope you found it helpful and that it inspires you to further frugal heights!

Love, Daisy

Printed in Great Britain
by Amazon

40922518R00195